# Lady Sunflower

## by Sierra Shuck-Sparer

stories, songs, and poems
from the desk of kill.gertrude

*chemo punch card*

*CANCER PLAYLIST PT. 1*

*HELL PILLS*

For Julia, Madeline, Jada, Lydia, Bennet, Jackson, and every other kid
who had to battle more than they should have.
I hope flowers bloom for you.

Quotes on pages 158-159 used with permission from Margaret Edson.

PAB-0609-0371 • ISBN: 978-1-4867-2986-9

Made in China/Fabriqué en Chine
Illustrated by Chloe Tyler and Sierra Shuck-Sparer

# Acknowledgements

There are so many people I want to thank that I don't even know where to begin. I guess I'll start with my rocks: all of the people that have helped me come this far. Thank you to my amazing family (especially my mom, who was the first to see this book in its larval state) who have driven me to appointments, held my hands during IV sticks, and watched Marvel and Disney movies with me on repeat. Thank you to my friends in Knoxville and Atlanta who have visited me in the hospital and continually supported and encouraged me through high school and college. Thank you to my West High and Georgia Tech teachers and administrators who have made my dual education-and-chemo possible and (relatively) manageable. Special shout-out to Anne Duvall from St. Jude and Jenny Weldon from KCS who made sure I was able to graduate high school on time. Thank you to all of my amazing nurses and doctors from Le Bonheur Children's Hospital, St. Jude Children's Research Hospital, East Tennessee Children's Hospital, Children's Healthcare of Atlanta, and (once) Oxford Children's Hospital, including (but not limited to) Dr. Boop, Dr. Gajjar, Dr. Aguilera, Dr. Spiller, Katie, and Ginger. Thank you Amanda for the Laffy Taffies, Kristin and Maggie for the PT, and Sandra for the massages. Thank you to my cancer coaches Kristen Gould and Beth Booker, and everyone else who has reached out to me and helped me beat back Gertrude. All of you are the reasons I was able to come this far.

For the publication of *Lady Sunflower*, I would like to thank the Make-A-Wish Foundation of East Tennessee, who fought through COVID to deliver my wish. Specifically, I would like to thank Christina Sayer who began the process, and Misty Parker who connected me to the editors and publishers who helped me make this wish a reality. Thank you to Flowerpot Press and Patrick Hayes for taking on my project, Katie Crow and Serena Isbell for refining *Lady Sunflower*, and the amazing Flowerpot artist team for the beautiful illustrations. I literally couldn't have done this without you! Thank you for making my wish come true and helping me and my book bloom!

# *Introduction*

No one expects to have a brain tumor. No one expects to meet their worst enemy either. I did both at once, before I was able to drive. Her name was Gertrude. But this is not her story.

When I was diagnosed with high-risk medulloblastoma, a type of brain cancer, I had just turned 15, meaning I was given the gift of sick kids: a Wish from Make-A-Wish.

I know the cliché Wish is a trip to Disney World or a celebrity meet-and-greet, and while both of those were tempting, I really wanted to go to Japan. Of course, I first had to get through the major brain surgery, 30 days of radiation, and seven months of chemotherapy that came after my diagnosis. And then, COVID-19 threw a wrench into everything, and I didn't hear back from Make-A-Wish for a while. When I did hear back, they said I couldn't leave the country anymore due to Ms. Rona, so I had to think of a new Wish.

I had already been writing thoughts and songs and such (mostly for therapy), so I decided that I wanted to write and publish a book about my cancer experience.

Then, just as I was finishing my senior year of high school, my cancer relapsed, and Gertrude returned. This time, with a new batch of drugs (and only a "minor" brain surgery), I was able to do chemo at home, in Knoxville, Tennessee, instead of six hours away in Memphis.

After the chemo summer, I started my first year at the Georgia Institute of Technology in Atlanta, Georgia. My second semester, I relapsed again and did chemo while staying full-time at GT. The whole time, I continued to write about everything, from emotions and the way I was feeling to more detailed descriptions of day-to-day life and treatments.

For *Lady Sunflower*, I wanted to include pieces from all five stages of my cancer treatment: the first diagnosis/treatment, the first break (no treatment), the second diagnosis/ treatment, the second break, and the third diagnosis/treatment, which brings us up to date. (At least, at the initial point of book creation. I've relapsed more times since, but that's for a later version.) Some of these pieces were created at different times than they are printed in, but I have arranged them in a way that makes sense with my headspace and evolution of my understanding of my treatment and myself.

This book has been many years in the making and I am excited to share it with you and continue to raise awareness about pediatric cancer. Let's kill Gertrude!

This is my story.

# Prologue

I was just beginning my sophomore year of high school when I met Gertrude, coming off a summer of hiking and camping through the Midwest, breaking personal swimming and rock-climbing records, working as a summer camp counselor-in-training, and making big ice skating progress. I was ready to take on my PSATs, three AP classes, and role as the vice president of my school's Gay-Straight Alliance (GSA).

Everything was going great, until one day in the middle of August, when I fell while ice skating. Don't get me wrong, I fell a lot. But in my (then) eight years of ice skating, I had never seriously hurt myself beyond a few bruises and strained muscles. This time, however, was different. I was doing a single loop (a pretty basic jump) when I caught a wrong edge and fell backwards. I didn't hit my head, but the whiplash was enough that my neck hurt. I didn't think anything of it, until we started doing twizzles in stroking class (basically ice skating aerobics), which involved spinning on one foot. I became incredibly dizzy, to the point that I fell over and my friend had to help me get off the ice. I sat until the world stopped spinning, then I got back on and forgot all about it.

A few days later, I had to get my physical exam from my pediatrician to participate in my high school's swimming and rock climbing teams. I was having a little bit of dizziness and headaches, and my doctor said I probably had a concussion, so I should wait a while before skating again. I took a break from sports, letting my head rest and go back to normal. Or so I thought.

After a few weeks, I tried to go back to skating, but while doing the Freestyle 4 dance pattern, I got dizzy again and fell. This was super frustrating because I was very close to passing Freestyle 4 (and getting to the level of learning axels) before my fall. No matter, I'll go swimming. The only problem there was that I would get so dizzy when breathing to the side that I had to pause in the middle of the lane until the world stopped spinning.

I was also having trouble with dizziness and headaches in school. I was having migraine-level headaches almost every day, exacerbated by the bright lights and loud halls. I had math class first thing in the morning, and although my grades weren't suffering for it, I often had to put my head down to avoid feeling dizzy.

My pediatrician recommended that I go to a neurologist to keep a closer eye on the concussion and make sure that it wasn't too serious and that it would get better. My neurologist basically just said that it looked like typical concussion symptoms and shouldn't be too much of a problem, despite me having a concussion once before. She sent me to a physical therapist who specialized in resetting ear crystals (a real thing, Google it) to fix vertigo, which is what my dizziness had escalated to at that point. The PT was kind of far away, but she was really nice, and the treatment seemed to be working. I flew to Minneapolis to see *Hamilton* with my mom that month.

But then, again, I started getting worse. I was constantly nauseous and dizzy, puking in the school's bathroom on my 15th birthday during Chemistry class. I would throw up at school, before and after my PT sessions, and while at the neurologist's office, and I lost a lot of weight because of it. Finally, the neurologist decided to order an MRI scan, just to make sure there wasn't something else worse going on in my brain.

The day of the MRI, I took the PSAT in my school's gym. My parents said I could stay home, but I had been preparing for it. It wasn't too bad. My head only hurt a little, thanks to the pain meds I took beforehand. My mom picked me up immediately after I finished the test, then we drove over to the children's hospital.

The MRI was supposed to be about 30 minutes long. I listened to *Hamilton* (I was obsessed at the time.). I knew something was wrong when we got to "Non-Stop."

The MRI technician and my mom came in a little bit after, and I got an IV. They didn't say much, just looked worried. The contrast wasn't too bad, it just tasted weird. I got to "The Election of 1800." It was late when we left. I don't remember what happened for the rest of the day.

The next morning, I slept in, missing school. When I came downstairs, my parents came in and told me that something was wrong and that I was going to need brain surgery.

This is when I learned about Gertrude.

# First

*October 2018 – August 2019*
*sophomore year*

After the MRI revealing Gertrude, I was rushed onto the schedule of one of the best brain surgeons in the world: Dr. Boop. My family and I went to Le Bonheur in Memphis, Tennessee for the procedure, then a week after surgery I was released to go to St. Jude Children's Research Hospital, where I met my primary oncology team and spent the next roughly eight months being treated for high-risk medulloblastoma brain cancer. I had 20 days of cranio-spinal proton radiation, 10 days of cranium radiation, and seven months of chemotherapy, alternating between known and experimental drugs as part of one of St. Jude's research programs. It was rough; I had to basically live in Memphis, in one of St. Jude's long-term housing facilities. Mom and Dad would switch out every other weekend to stay with me (one parent had to stay home with my brother, Aidan, who was 11 at the time). The chemo itself was pretty harsh, making me lose my hearing, strength, appetite, and ankle strength. This section covers everything from my original diagnosis to finally reaching NED (No Evidence of Disease) status.

### Screw You, Gertrude

*a song for my tumor with Panic! At The Disco-style music*


me: Doctor?
doctor: That MRI that you had yesterday
me: Yes?
doctor: There's something strange, and this is hard to say, but…
me: What?

doctor:
Well I don't want to scare you,
But there's something there you
Know that should just be brain tissue.
Well you see over here, now,
There's no need to fear now,
But this is certainly an issue.

So here's what you do: You go to Memphis,
They'll cut it out and see what it is

me:
So that's what I do, I go to Memphis
To Memphis

So I showed, unprepared,
And I laid down, feeling scared,
And when I woke up, I'd lost my hair.

Having surgery
Crying in my sleep
I've got 3 IVs

Feeling dizzy
Eye patched so I can see
What has it done to me?

So screw you, Gertrude

me: Doctor?
doctor: We got most of her, that's fair to say
me: Yes?
doctor: But she has spread, she didn't go away
me: What?

doctor:
Well I don't want to scare you,
But since she's still there you
will have to stay with us
Your parents can live here,
It's only for one year
You will just have to readjust

So here's what you do: radiation and chemo
They'll zap her out and make sure she's gone

me:
So that's what I do: radiation and chemo
And chemo

So I showed up, unprepared,
And I laid down, feeling scared,
When I woke up, I'd lost my hair

Chemotherapy
Fevers in my dreams
No more radiation please

Messed up chemistry
Feeling hard to breathe
What has it done to me?

So screw you, Gertrude

I don't want your prayers, I don't want your thoughts
I've got a 60% chance, and that's not a lot
Please don't tell me that I have got spirit
I don't want to hear it, I don't want to hear it no, no, no

I don't care if it's cool here; I want to go home
I want you to visit, I can't be alone
Please don't tell me there's no need to fear it
I don't want to hear it, I don't want to hear it no

(*slower*)
I know I have acted strong
Pretended like nothing is wrong
I guess that's why I wrote this song

Will I live to see
Next year or next week?
What'll become of me?

So screw you, Gertrude.

## overheard

"Mommy it's scary."
I heard a kid say this today.
He had a whine in his voice as he reached for her hand.
"Mommy it's scary."
The monsters under his bed keep him up at night. They make me cry, too.
"Mommy it's scary."
They had to draw blood from him that day. I saw the family was headed that way.
"Mommy it's scary."
It's scary to be sedated, while high doses of chemicals and radiated beams kill off all of the cells that keep him alive. I chose to conquer radiation without sedation, but little kids like him have no choice. They can't stay still for that long.

"Mommy it's scary."
"It's not scary," she replies gently, picking him up and hugging him tight.
She faces her own monsters.
While the kid faces pain, she faces the possibility of never being able to see him again.
Of watching him cry out in pain, and then never cry out again. She stays brave for this kid, for her child, whom she loves. She stays brave to show him that it's not scary. He doesn't understand. Cancer doesn't discriminate between ages, races, classes, genders, mental stabilities.

"I'm scared."

I want to say this, but they are dealing with their own monsters.

"I'm scared."

I'm scared of the blood draws that make me vomit.

I'm scared of the radiation that makes me lose my hair and my appetite.

I'm scared of chemotherapy and falling behind in school.

I'm scared of tomorrow and the unknown.

I'm scared of living. I'm scared of dying.

"It's not scary."

# beginning vs the end

What am I going to do today!
The children excitedly say
In this new place with these new friends
And all the games we'll play!

What do I have to do today?
The children tiredly say
All of the fun has disappeared
And the joy has gone away.

# Lady Sunflower

Lady Sunflower, standing tall,
Rises above to shield them all,
Heaven forbid her petals fall
And allow her feelings to show.

Lady Sunflower, full of grace,
Never shows a cloudy face,
Knows that life is not a race
But feels behind even so.

Lady Sunflower, sugar and spice,
Always tries to behave nice,
Sends the cat to catch the mice
But when they do, she'll always feel low.

Lady Sunflower sweetly swings,
About cloudless days and butterfly wings,
Who could ever want other things?
She does but hides it below.

Lady Sunflower, stuck in bed,
Droopy leaves and propped-up head,
Gets frustrated but never turns red,
She hides it under her yellow.

## *Energy Charts*

### how I feel (mentally)

how I feel (physically)

| | Terrible | OK | pretty good |
|---|---|---|---|
| Terrible | No focus | Some focus | Some focus |
| OK | no focus | good focus | laser focus |
| pretty good | No focus | laser focus | great day |

↳ based on this:

| Level of focus | → | activity |
|---|---|---|
| No focus | → | watch a movie that I've seen already |
| some focus | → | watch a new movie or show |
| good focus | → | organize / clean up |
| laser focus | → | make clay, art, or earrings, read a book |
| great day | → | do multiple of the above! maybe even drive somewhere! |

$$y = mi + (sick)$$
$$if\ (time) \geq \infty \longrightarrow help$$

$$(si)(ck) = -(up\ for\ it)$$

if $x = [+walking]$ and $y = [-energy]$, $xy \neq happening$

### percentages of days spent doing stuff

a day with chemo
- sleeping
- watching movies
- eating

a day with no chemo
- making art
- reading
- walking / going to the park
- cleaning / organizing

### comparing the energy levels of days on chemo with days off chemo

- days off chemo
- days on chemo

energy level

\# days

# *do you realize how much you value your hair?*

Do you realize how much you value your hair?
How reliant you are on its shape and texture to bring personality to your face,
To be able to express yourself.

Or even, to keep your head warm during the winter
And to keep your head from getting sunburnt during the summer.

Do you realize how often you brush your fingers through your hair,
Feeling the strands untangle and smooth,
As your hair blows in the winds and shines in the sun.

Do you think about what it would be like to have no hair?
To look at yourself in the mirror and see nothing but skin,
When your hair should be growing but it's not
And you know that it's because your body is hurting.

Think about it.

## *losing hair*

When you lose your hair
(Due to radiation but more likely chemo)
You lose <u>all</u> of your hair.

This house has
No drapes (to keep the light out)
No carpets (to keep your feet warm)
No bed sheets (to hold you close at night)
No blankets (to keep you sheltered)
No clothes (to keep you comfortable)
No cloths (to fill in the gaps).

A bare bones, a freezing house,
That gets new clothes once the cold is gone.
But in the meantime, it shivers.

*eyelashes pt. 1*

You don't realize it,
Because it's often not the worst Thing
And therefore not the Thing that gets talked about,
But when the chemicals start working,
And one finds themselves going bald,
The eyelashes are the last to fall
And when they do, they go
E v e r y w h e r e
Which is irritating on its own,
But most importantly,
They poke your eyes as they fall out,
One last act of defiance,
Before they join their fallen comrades
And are swept up.

## reflux (and nausea)

*(to the tune of "Turkey in the Straw" aka "Is Your Cat Kinda Fat")*

*reflux*
Is
Your

Chest on fire
Does your throat feel like it's drier
Do you choke on all your food
Does it cause a bad mood
Can you feel the heartburn
Can you hear the stomach churn

Is your
Chest
On
Fire

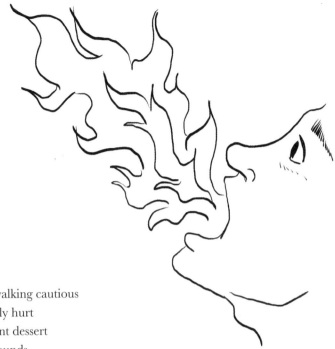

*nausea*
Do
You

Feel really nauseous
Does it make your walking cautious
Does your head really hurt
Do you not even want dessert
Do you lose a few pounds
Do your smiles turn to frowns

Do you
Feel
Really
Nauseous

## *Week 4*

Treatment comes in four-week cycles
With doses on one and three
The second one isn't quite as bad
(At least that's what they're telling me).

So when it's time for me to have
A break from this languor,
I always will look forward to
The peace brought by Week 4.

This is a time I can relax
With no radiation or chemo
When all I have to do is heal
And enjoy the *bellissimo*.

Usually this is when my friends
Come to join me in my suite
And now I know I surely will
My nemesis defeat.

## *the soldier*

The soldier fights the toughest wars
Endures the suffering and horrors
She camps at night upon the shores
Of an island made of her pain.

The soldier wishes she was done
But knows she can't leave 'til the war is won
She should have known when she begun
About what's behind those doors.

The soldier wishes she could train
Against the struggles and the strain
As she sings the final, last refrain
There's nothing she can outrun.

## the Decadron Song

*(in the style of Bo Burnham with jazzy piano accompaniment)*

*(slower)*
The medical name is Dexamethasone
But the cool kids call it "Dex"
If this is where we're starting,
I can't wait to see what happens next

'Cause I'm on this medication
That's made of Devil's spawn
You know the one I'm talking about—
Decadron

Oh lord, I hate it

*(faster)*
It speeds up my heart
And it slows down my eyes
My stomach is bloated,
Got new weight in my thighs

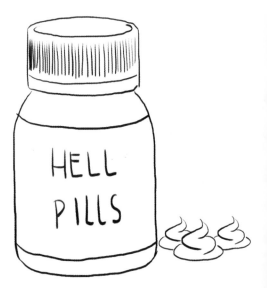

It makes my hands real shaky
And my knees and ankles achy
And I wake up every night in a cold sweat
Now, why can't I get off the Decadron yet?

They've been weaning it down each and every day,
But I kinda just wish that they'd take it away
I don't want to think that it's here to stay, 'cause
Oh lord! I really hate Decadron

It makes my face real puffy
And every room real stuffy
And I can't get enough of any food that I eat
The road is getting tough-y
But I'll eat those mini muffies
And I'll put those fuzzy socks right onto my feet

I forgot about the good things it's supposed to do
'Cause it's making it harder for me to go…through with treatment

I gotta stick it out
Even though I want to shout:
Take me off of the Decadron!

I'm sure I'm as miserable as I can get,
But I probably haven't discovered half of the side effects yet
Oh lord! I really hate Decadron

# *where do cancers come from?*

Where do cancers come from?

Well,

some come from outside sources, called *carcinogens*.

These are things that cause cancers to develop because they are harmful to your body's cells.

These include:

- Asbestos, which was used in some old houses' vinyl tiles, wallpaper, and insulation.
  When the connection between asbestos and cancer was made, people developed ways of
  removing the asbestos from houses safely.
- Radiation, like the kind used in nuclear warfare or in nuclear power plants. When the US
  bombed Japan to end World War II, the landscape continued to retain the radiation from
  the bombs and still causes citizens to experience cancer development and other negative
  side effects. A nuclear power plant is very dangerous but is very successful at producing
  energy. Nuclear power plants have to be careful about containing radiation and not letting
  any escape.

  > *The radiation used by oncologists to treat cancer are smaller doses so they are not super
  > harmful to the body. They are also very specific and able to target only the areas of the
  > body that contain cancer. Proton radiation is more specific than photon radiation, so ask
  > for that if you have a choice. Oncologists know when is the best time to use either one to
  > treat a cancer. Also, there is a limit to how much radiation your body will receive before
  > it starts being harmed by the treatments. Oncologists will know when that is.

- The sun when its rays are absorbed in high quantities. The sun's beams actually contain
  radiation (known as ultraviolet rays), however, they are only harmful if you are exposed to
  a lot of them. This is why it is very important to protect your skin with sunscreen when you
  go outside. The more radiation your skin absorbs, the more likely your skin cells are to
  mutate into cancer later in your life. This radiation can also come from tanning beds.
- Cigarettes, specifically the tobacco in them. When the connection between cigarettes and
  cancer was made, the government ordered cigarette companies to disclose the harmful
  effects of cigarettes, but overall did little to stop them beyond that because of corruption
  and bribery by the Big Tobacco companies. More recent campaigns about the health
  risks of cigarettes (as well as many buildings developing smoke-free zones) have reduced
  the consumption of cigarettes, and the likelihood of second-hand smoke inhalation causing
  bystanders to develop cancer has declined.

Some things that *do not* cause cancer include:
- Windmills
- Watching television
- Microwaves (even though they use radiation to cook your food, the wavelengths are not strong enough to affect your cells), radio waves

Some cancers are hereditary. This means that they are passed from mother or father to the child through their genes. These include breast cancer, colon cancer, and prostate cancer. This is why it is very important that, as you get older, you get regularly checked for these cancers, especially if you know that someone in your family has had one before. If you catch a cancer early, you may be able to remove it with surgery instead of having to also go through chemo and radiation.

Some cancers occur just because something goes wrong in the DNA replicating process of your cells. Sometimes these cells mutate and become fast-growing, fast-replicating, cell-consuming tumors that grow and attempt to take over your bodily processes. These are the most unexpected cancers and are generally unpreventable.

No, it's not a punishment.
No, you don't deserve it.
Yes, there is a low chance of getting cancer.
Yes, there is a lower chance of dying from cancer.
Yes, someone has to make the statistics.
No, there's no way it's you.

# *Why I Don't Believe in God*

I don't believe in God.

My reasoning: Why would anyone, all-powerful or not, create Pediatric Cancer?

What Otherworldly Being would say, "You know what, we are going to create a flaw in the human genome so complex that it takes chemicals and radiation beams to treat the resulting ruthless mass of uncontrollable cells. And, let's make these treatments super harsh on the body and mind. Like, it'll-knock-you-out levels of bad. And, let's not make it purely physical. Let's spiral people down a dark depressed hole because their body isn't theirs to control. But also, this shouldn't just happen to adults who have sinned, or those who are old and ready to die, or people in a mentally/physically stable area of life where they can handle going through treatments. You know who my 'soldiers' should be? Kids. No age is too young (yes, babies too!). And, let's also make it kind of common. Just for the heck of it. Sounds right."

Someone once told me, "God picks His strongest soldiers for His toughest battles."

Ok, but why did He choose cancer as His battle? And why did He choose babies, toddlers, tweens, and teens as His soldiers?

Does He realize how much cancer treatment messes up these kids' lives?

Is it part of His big plan to make them suffer?

I do understand why, when faced with these momentous challenges, people choose to turn to God for comfort and salvation. I get it, I don't think less of you for it. It does seem easier to believe that it will All Work Out, that Everything Happens For A Reason. It takes a lot of work to think about how life is more complicated than a bumper sticker slogan or a singular verse from a lengthy text.

Sometimes it helps to boil it down. Condense a life's worth of lessons and beliefs into a single rule that will direct everything into place. It's nice to rely on Other Things to figure out messes and uncomplicate situations.

When the pressure is gone to do the things that will affect your life (because, hey, someone else is in charge), there is some relief, at least for those who believe the pressure is truly gone. I feel like I have done enough chemo and school that I need that pressure to make sure I can keep up. It is exhausting. But it doesn't make me a believer.

I don't keep up in school because Someone wills it. I don't thank Whoever for the days when I don't throw up. Oncologists didn't discover chemo because of Divine Intervention. My tumors don't get smaller by the grace of the Universe.

And, why kids? It always comes back to kids.

Why would Someone Above bring a being into the world, an "image-bearer" if you would, only to poison their body and doom them to not know adulthood. Frozen in time, whisked off the face of the earth before they've truly taken steps into it.

For those of you who have told me you will pray for me (and for kids like me), thank you for helping me in the way that you know best.

But after everything I've seen and everything I've been through, I don't believe in God.

However, believer or not, all cancer patients should go to heaven, so in the afterlife they can do all of the things that they never got to do on Earth. They have to—so they can make up for their lost lives.

## *scary*

One of the scariest things I have ever experienced was when I almost had to get my port out in the middle of treatment.

It was 2019. I think I had two or three months of IV chemo left. When you're a cancer patient, your immune cells die off because of the chemo, which is why cancer patients need to be careful to not get sick. A pretty standard part of the chemo I was on was the increased risk of having a dangerous temperature spike as a result of an infection or something else also bad.

Sometimes, it happens for literally no reason. But when it does happen (and it has to be higher than a certain threshold) it's a fire drill.

1. "Mom/Dad, I don't feel very well"
2. Take your temperature (it's high)
3. Lay on the couch feeling dizzy and bad while Mom/Dad packs the Go Bag (which is almost completely ready to go, but they throw some extra socks/barf bags/blankets in there)
4. Ride in a wheelchair (and in a haze)
5. Mom/Dad drives us over to St. Jude (about a 5 minute drive)
6. Go inside, to the Medicine Room (because high temperatures always happen late at night, and Assessment Triage isn't open past 7:00 p.m.)
7. Nurse takes my temperature (sometimes higher, sometimes the same, sometimes lower)
8. Get a Tylenol while the nurses assemble
9. Get port accessed + nurses draw IV blood culture samples as well
      - They draw from both sites to make sure the port isn't infected
      - I am a really hard IV stick and the rooms are always cold and I'm usually dehydrated, so it's not fun
10. Wait a bit to see if there is anything wrong/to see if the temperature goes down
11. [Usually] get admitted into inpatient hospital care
      - This could be because they found something, but usually it was because I either had more inpatient chemo coming, or because I needed a blood or treatment infusion and it was late at night.
12. Wait to see if my cultures grow anything that we need to worry about (usually they don't)

Even though fevers are usually just little annoyances, sometimes they can be indicative of something that actually needs to be treated.

This time, I was in the middle of a rough cycle. I had to go into the Med Room very late at night. I was moved inpatient, had to go through the whole process at some ungodly hour. Then, the oncologist and her nurse practitioner came in at 7:00 in the morning for rounds.

I am barely awake, mentally and physically tired, feeling sick already, when they told me, "We found infection in your port. We are going to have to remove it."

This was terrible because (a) I'm almost done with chemo and (b) I would have to take everything (transfusions, IV medicines, chemos) through an IV. I don't do well with IVs. I have rolly, tiny veins. I sometimes puke or come close to passing out. They start hurting within 24 hours after getting them.

I started crying, and the doctor said, "You've been such a trooper, I'm so sorry."

I just said, "I'm tired of trooping." Because I was.

They drew more port cultures just to make sure there was something they needed to remove the port for, or to see if their earlier sample had been contaminated.

In the end, I didn't have to get my port removed. But the whole experience was super scary.

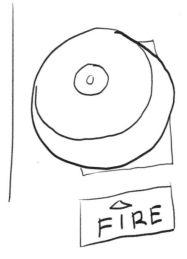

## the chemo spa

*(to the tune of "Welcome to the Internet" by Bo Burnham)*

Welcome to the Chemo Spa!
I heard you want to try
Baby soft new skin, new hair and
Lashes on your eyes.

We've got millions of treatments
(No better, all worse)
If you don't feel the difference after,
You'd be the first.

Welcome to the Chemo Spa!
I heard you want new abs
All you have to do is puke
And get more IV jabs.

You want to get rid of calluses?
Step in our machine
Radiation does the trick
To wipe your skin clean.

Welcome to the Chemo Spa!
You want to lose some pounds?
Try our new diet (called chemo),
You don't even move around.

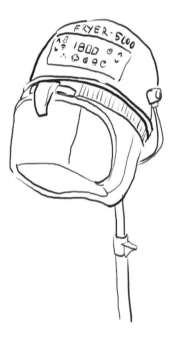

You want time off of classes?
Some time to relax?
We can give this to you
But you won't get time back.

Could I interest you in getting sick
All of the time?
A chance to stay at home and binge
All of the time?
Your skin and your hair replaced
All of the time?
Could I interest you in being sick
All of the time?

Welcome to the Chemo Spa.

*(evil laughter)*

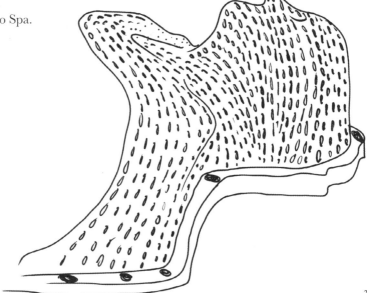

## *thief*

She sneaks around in the darkness of night,
Hiding in shadows, just out of sight
You might catch a glimpse, but only slight
For She knows the ways of the dark.

Look out, for She seeks to take
The memories and summer break
You don't realize just what's at stake
Or how long She will leave her mark.

But you must be warier still
Of the sickness waves and nausea chill
Of the grainy, chalky, yucky pill
When blood's in the water, She's a shark.

Oh, how I often curse fate
That She is here, spreading hate
That I'm resigned to not swim, run, or skate
Her cruel thievery is stark.

## *the waiting song*

*(with piano accompaniment, getting gradually faster)*

We
Sit and wait and sit and wait
And sit and wait to sit and wait
Then sit and wait and sit and wait and sit and wait some more

'Til
The nurse comes in and calls my name
And we go in but still the same
We sit and wait and sit and wait and sit and wait again now

The door opens but it's just to check
So we sit and wait (and what the heck!)
We sit and wait and sit and wait some more now

Hurry up to sit and wait
Then go on in to sit and wait
Then stay right here to sit and wait and my butt's getting sore now

*(slower)*
Oh, the doctor is just now coming in
I do my best to bear it and give her my brightest grin
And oh, she says (much to my chagrin),
"You're done waiting and it's time to now begin."

## *A Breakup Letter*

Dear Gertrude,

You have entered the wrong head, my friend. I bet you didn't realize when you set up shop
and started messing with my brain that mine is the mind of a fighter, a pusher, a go-getter.
Someone too stubborn to say "I can't do it," and so I do it. I am someone who dismisses
doubts and walks on clouds. You thought I was easy, like you could take me over without a
complaint, but I am not ready to give in to your dizzy spells and whims and greedy fantasies.
When I first met you, you were only a whisper in my ears and a pain behind my eyes, but then
you grew, disguised with good intentions and a little bit of vertigo. It took a while to see what
you truly were. And we talked and laughed and spoke normally, so I thought you were fine.
You wormed your way inside and gained my trust. You told me lies and made it hard to think
and concentrate around the fluff you stuffed in my skull. You made it hard to stand up and get
out of bed. You occupied my every thought and weighed me down, even as I lost weight.
This is me breaking up with you, Gertrude. We are never getting back together, like ever.
Because what you didn't realize is that I will never break. My mind is set and I don't need you.
I can live without you. I live better without you. You may have messed up the beginning of my
year, but you are just a word in the essay of my life. Whiteout will fix any blemishes you leave
behind. Screw you, Gertrude.

Sincerely,
Me

## Limericks

There once was a girl named Sierra
Who sat down in the wrong chair-a
When the needle went in
The world began to spin
And then she lost all of her hair-a

There once was a tumor named Gertrude
Who was very picky with her food
She chomped on my brain,
Causing quite a great pain,
So in chemo drugs she was then stewed

There once was a medulloblastoma
(Not to confuse with sarcoma)
She studied real hard
Leaving my head all scarred
In order to earn her diploma

### *Alternate ending (for when I feel better)*
*(softer)*


My chemotherapy
Is over—now I'm
free I won't let her
stop me

I'll stand down for nobody
I'm gonna get my college degree
I've got a world to see

I'll be who I want to be
Loving every day and every week
I'm living life, and that's all me

So screw you, Gertrude.

## *Break* (1)

*September 2019 – March 2021
junior year to spring of senior year*

Even though I had gotten no evidence of disease, I was still having to go back to St. Jude every three months for scans. I was feeling the effects of the chemo in how I now needed hearing aids and how weak I was. I was able to swim again, but not as fast as I had been able to before, and I was able to ice skate, but dizziness was a big issue. I was getting frustrated, but I still appreciated being free from the hospital. I kept getting better by acknowledging my weakness and not letting it hold me down. I was on a swim team again, and I raised over $7,000 for St. Jude by making and selling origami earrings. Also, I was in my senior year, about to graduate from high school! 2020 was a great year (for me). I was able to get my port out, and I was about to be able to have St. Jude scan appointments further apart. Everything was going pretty well. Whew.

## *a break*

Have you ever taken time off from something?
Something that you've been doing your whole life
(Or maybe even for just a little while),
And you come back feeling wobbly, unsteady, a little bit weak.
But your body remembers what it felt like,
So you know you can get back
To where you were.

Ok. Now.

Imagine that, during your time off,
You got chemicals
Pushed into your body
(In large enough quantities to get past the brain's barriers),
Large enough that your nurse practitioner shudders
When she thinks of Just How Much she has to prescribe.
Large enough that you lose 25 pounds toward an unhealthy weight
And you lose your hearing and your strength to walk.

And you feel the break.
It breaks your body, head, heart.
It breaks your love of that thing, breaks the good memories you have of it.
And you feel empty.

Meanwhile, everyone you have grown up with doing the thing
Has moved on without you, left you behind.
And they don't understand why you don't feel like doing it anymore
Because you have been doing it for a while.

But they don't understand how
Soul crushing,
Heart wrenching,
Mind reeling
It feels to suddenly feel so weak and so behind
In something you used to be good at.

A break leaving you broken.
It's not the same as taking time off.

## *put a finger down (TikTok style)*

Put a finger down if you spent nine years of your life since you were six learning how to ice skate and then you got pretty good at it and you devoted a lot of your time to it, and then one day when you were doing some normal exercises you fell doing a fairly simple jump and then you got a concussion from the whiplash of falling so you tried to take it easy to help your brain heal, but the dizziness and concussion symptoms kept getting worse every week to the point where you were having daily migraine-like headaches and nausea/vomiting spells, and then you had to see a special ear-crystal-correcting physical therapist which helped for a while, but when it had been almost three months since the original fall, your neurologist finally decides that you should get an MRI, but when they do, they discover a high-risk cancerous brain tumor about the size of a baseball that needs as-soon-as-possible brain surgery by a well-known brain surgeon six hours away in Memphis, Tennessee later that week, which then leads to many months of chemotherapy treatments and a complete upheaval of your life and wellbeing.

*puts finger down*

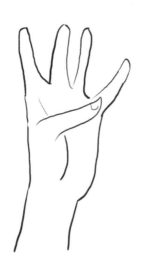 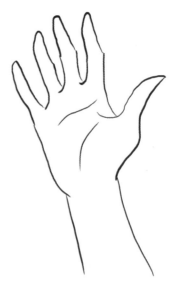

*I often wish the world would stop and wait for me to get better, but it never does.*

# *every three months*

It is not a bad place
But when I look around
And see the bald heads
And hear the babies cry
And feel the silent sickness
And taste the lack of appetite
And know the probabilities
It is hard not to be afraid

*a fun fact about me*

I'm always paranoid about whether or not I flushed the toilet because when I was at St. Jude, all of the toilets were automatic, so I never had to flush, and now I am worried that I forget to flush. I never forget, but I always go back to check.

## *Let It Go*

*(to the tune of "Let Her Go" by Passenger \*not Frozen\*)*

Well, you only miss your strength when you're feeling weak
Only miss the past when the future's bleak
Only moving on once you've let it go
Only know you were good once your strength is gone
Only feel unlucky when the sticks are drawn
Only moving on once you've let it go.

Staring out the window at the cars
Wondering when this had to get so hard
But you're so close, you've made it so far

You think about it before you fall asleep
So wrapped up that you can't even count sheep
Your every mistake, they cut so deep.

'Cause you only hate yourself when you wonder why
Only realize when you start to cry
Hard to move on if you can't let it go
Only feel alone with no one to hold
Thinking that this cancer thing is getting old
Trying to move on but you can't let it go

So hard to let it go.

## *eyelashes pt. 2*

When you are all better,
When the chemo is done,
And your hair starts to recover,
Starts to grow back in
Soft fluffy patches,
Your eyelashes come back.

But they come back slowly.
So painfully slow,
I get so irritated thinking about
How long and dark they used to be.

And when they grow back,
They don't know how.
They try to point inward,
Poking my eye again.
Pain going out and pain coming back.

I had to go to an eye doctor
For her to use tweezers to
Carefully, slowly
Twist them, guide them
In the right direction.

With a little help, they grew fine.

## *cancer fun facts in rhyme*

Fun fact and trivia time!
Listen now and answer the rhyme—

---

Here's some science, see if you can list them,
This part's all about the immune and blood system!

When your cells divide at very high rates,
This creates cancer if the cell…mutates!

Cancer treatment targets cells that multiply quickly,
That's why it knocks you out and makes you feel…sickly!

Knocked-out cells are the ones that you know:
Platelets, reds, and also…bone marrow!

---

Find and pair the meds and effects.
Hold on now 'cause it might get complex!

Vincristine's a drug that lives up to the talk,
I took it once and soon couldn't…walk!

Marinol's a med only some people need,
Its closest relative is basically…weed!

Cisplatin's a chemo that everyone's fearing,
I had it IV, and then lost my…hearing!

---

This last section's all about being a patient
Listen closely to answer how all of my days went!

This never worked, its sting was like bees
My veins did not work well with…IVs!

Unfortunately this feeling was never a fluke
Because all I would feel was the strong urge to…puke!

These last days of the cycle always made me want more
That's because the best time I had was during week…four!

# How I Killed Gertrude
## (my college application essay)

The summer of 2018 was the Best Summer Ever: road trips, rock climbing in Yosemite, a counselor-in-training position at summer camp, and new personal records in swimming and ice skating. All in all, I was on top of the world.

Then, my world turned upside down.

I named my high-risk medulloblastoma brain tumor Gertrude. The weeks after her discovery were crazy and disorienting. Six days after the initial MRI, I had brain surgery. Seven days after that, I moved to St. Jude Children's Research Hospital in Memphis, Tennessee for radiation and chemotherapy. I could not tell what was worse—lying on a metal table for two hours for radiation, enduring chemotherapy that made me nauseous and caused permanent hearing loss, or being far away from everything I knew and loved.

Throughout nearly a year of treatment, I tried to channel my experience into art and school. I started an Instagram account called "kill.gertrude" to keep a photo journal of my cancer journey, which included MRI memes and barf-bag hats. I created art based on my treatments, like "The ABCs of Craniospinal Radiation" and "The Decadron Song." I was also determined to keep up with schoolwork. I wanted to finish my classes, take my exams, and begin my junior year. The week of AP exams, I was hospitalized with a lung infection. I didn't let that stop me; I took one exam, had lung surgery, then took the next exam.

On August 23, 2019, I had my last chemo infusion. On September 10, I was officially declared cancer-free, and done with treatment. Five days later, I was home. With the help of my friends, family, and amazing medical staff, I had killed Gertrude.

Getting through cancer was hard, but living after it was even harder. I guess I had assumed that once I was home, everything would be fine and I would feel normal again. But for the next three months, I continued to struggle with nausea, and I still had to wear leg braces and hearing aids. I didn't feel like going to a full day of school, and I didn't feel like getting back into any of my athletic activities. It was frustrating—being this close to a normal life but still not having the strength to live it. I tried to do everything I had done before Gertrude, but it was so much harder than I had ever imagined.

So, I took baby steps. I went to physical therapy until I was strong enough to swim a mile. I went to ice skating lessons until I was steady on my feet. I went to classes one by one until I could handle a full day of school. I made and sold origami earrings until I raised $7,050 to begin to thank St. Jude for saving my life. I learned to be comfortable in my skin. Gertrude showed me how much I had not appreciated about life and how determined I am to live it.

Now I want to help other people live too. I was inspired by the doctors and nurses who helped me; I want to be like them. St. Jude's comprehensive care and no out-of-pocket-payment healthcare system is exactly what I want to bring to other communities.

I plan to major or minor in public policy and cellular biology, and then go to medical school. I want to specialize in providing aid and medical treatment to low-income communities. I want to work with the political system to help make healthcare easier to navigate and easier to access. I want to give others the security, knowledge, and care that St. Jude gave me.

Gertrude changed my life. At 15, my world fell apart. At 16, I put it back together. Now, at 17, I want to make a difference in the world of healthcare.

## The Girl Who Loved the World

There once was a girl who loved the world.

She loved daffodils in the spring, and crunchy leaf piles in the fall, and petting cats, and doing puzzles, and making art.
She would climb up mountains, and paddle down rivers, and spin without getting dizzy.
When she would jump, she would fly.

The girl loved the world.

But one day, the girl got sick. Really sick.
The kind of sick that takes you away from your home, that makes you lose your hair, and that takes a long, long time to get better.

She started to dislike the world.

She didn't like feeling crummy on sunny days and not being able to eat her favorite foods.
She didn't like being far from her friends and her cat. But most of all, she didn't like being unable to do anything because she was always too tired.

She felt mad.
She felt sad.
She felt angry, and she would scream when no one was around.

The girl hated the world.

But what she didn't know was that while she was feeling bad, the world was calling people to help make her feel better.

They sent letters and messages, flowers and teddy bears, love and support.
They held her heavy head and let her know that they would always be there for her, no matter how tired, mad, sad, or angry she felt.

The girl still felt sick, but with the support of the world behind her, she knew she could get better.

It took a while, but the girl came to love the world again.
And the world loved her, too.

## Second

*March 2021 – August 2021*
*second part of senior year*

I relapsed, unexpectedly, in March of my senior year of high school, just before prom, graduation, and my high school's musical performances of *Bright Star*, in which I was an ensemble member. I just remember crying in the oncologist's office. My oncologist said I could wait until after the *Bright Star* performances were over to begin chemotherapy. So, I had a "minor" brain surgery the week of my spring break before heading back to school. After I had performed in the last show, my parents and I drove to Memphis for chemo the next day. I had the first dose at St. Jude, then the others at East Tennessee Children's Hospital, about ten minutes away from my house. It was nice to not be on the other side of the state, but the chemo itself was still pretty rough. But, the way that the schedule was laid out, I could still go to prom and graduation. So I did.

## *relapse*

I guess they always say an end
Is a new beginning—time's friend
When doors close and windows open,
But they never tell you how to hope when
On any given, particular day,
The beginning goes the other way.

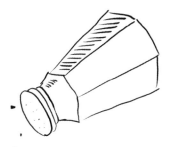

## *just a little salty*

There are no happy endings
The good guy never wins
They always pause on happy notes
But that's when the bad begins

There are no pots of gold
At the ends of rainbows
There's just a heap of mud
And that's where poison ivy grows

There are no healthy people
In the world of cancers
You get out once, but something's wrong
And no one's got the answers

I have to start all over
So yeah I'm a bit mad
I've done my time, I've paid my dues
But I guess that's just too bad!

## the soldier (pt. 2)

The soldier leaves victorious
Thinks that she is done, I guess
But little does she know that her success
Will outrun her in the long term

The soldier doesn't even know
The length that she will have to go
To fight to see the winter snow
That the break is just a recess

The hard rock ground is now unfirm
Eaten by the cruel tapeworm
A parasite that continues to squirm
Could she ever escape from this mess?

# *topotecan haikus*

[Day 1]
Meds before it starts:
Benadryl and Phenergan
Sleep through infusion

[Day 2]
Pretty much the same
Appetite is going down
Rely on smoothies

[Day 3]
Unremarkable
That's what we want days to be
Patient outpatient

[Day 4]
Spreading down my chest
An ugly set of freckles
Bright red and itchy

[Day 5]
We knew it would spike,
But my fever always would
Surprise my nurses

## *starting the next cycle*

This is my last day of feeling alright
When the sun is out and my future's bright
When I go to bed and see the stars at night
This is my last night of feeling alright

This is my last day of feeling good
When food tastes and smells as it should
When flowers bloom in the darkest wood
This is my last day of feeling good

This is my last day of feeling okay
When I can sit outside and the world isn't gray
When I can breathe the air and I'm able to say
"I will have another day of feeling okay"

YOU ARE NOW LEAVING:
NORMAL LIFE

### *how are you feeling today?*

Today I'm feeling a tad bit
Hysterical
If I have to answer another question from
Someone who means well

If I ignore them because I've answered too many ones like them today
Surely they will feel bad, and then that's on me; then I feel bad

How do I say that I feel
Outnumbered by people
Who want to hear how I feel?

I don't know how to say it nicely because everyone means well, and that's not bad

Feelings are complicated
Everyone knows that
Everyone wants to help me untangle them but please
Let me just sit here in my own bubble today.

## *journal 5-20-21*

I don't feel this way a lot. But lately I've been feeling it more.

It might just be the lack of blood in my body, or lack of food in my stomach, or the numbness in my face, or my inability to retain fluids, or my brain's imminent shutdown. It's been all that before.

One time, when my bed was still over where the bookshelves are now (so maybe seventh or eighth grade?), I felt this way. I think I had a nightmare about it the night before. But I woke up, and I was convinced. It was going to be a car crash, I think. As the day went on, the dream got foggier and foggier, until it wasn't in the front of my mind. But I guess it never went away, because I'm thinking of it now.

I think I felt this way during the first round of treatment. I must've, surely. But it's hard to remember because of the way that I dulled the experience down and shined it up for college essays. Repeat "it wasn't hard" over and over, and then that becomes true, if you don't think about it enough. Anyway.

Therapists and doctors ask, "Are you thinking about self-harm? Killing yourself?" That's the question. And yeah, it makes sense, especially when you look at the number of people that have killed themselves. But I don't.

I don't because I know how much there is to see. Or maybe I don't, really, but I want to see it. I do want to live. I want to live as much as I can.

So, that's the thought I've been having. It's a really hard thought to stop thinking. I know it's only Week 2, that I will be feeling better next week and the week after. I know that I have the chance of getting better. It's hard to think that I have only two weeks before this all starts again. And, while that's happening, I'll have scans to see if this is working. If any of what we've been doing has actually been fighting the cancer that's killing me.

I think I'm going to die.

I'll talk to my therapist tomorrow.

## *when a half becomes a third*

When a half becomes a third,
You lose about a sixth
Which doesn't seem like very much
When you've got nothing to compare it with

But if you sit for just a moment
And really think about it
What once was four, now is six
And that's much more, don't doubt it

Especially if you were halfway done
With something that would be done on time
But now you're only at one-third
Additional sentence for the same crime

I know that in the end it's good
To have an extra third
But it still hurts all the same
When I'm condemned by one word

The name that haunts me in my dreams
And keeps me up at night
Who rudely crushes all my hopes
And tells me I won't be alright.

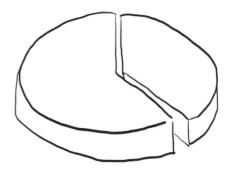

## *Chemo Town*

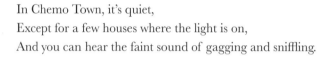

In Chemo Town, it's quiet,
Except for a few houses where the light is on,
And you can hear the faint sound of gagging and sniffling.

In Chemo Town, people walk slow with their heads down,
They don't go outside because it's never sunny,
But even if it was sunny, they couldn't go outside because of their sensitive skin.

People in Chemo Town used to do things.
But Chemo Town has a way of making people
Not like the things they used to.

Chemo Town people never work,
Or if they do, they don't do much,
They can't concentrate, their visions blur.

Nobody wants to live in Chemo Town,
Most people move out after a few months, and
A few stay for years, or at least have to come back to visit.

Chemo Town people can't choose to leave;
They are tied down by cords and strings.
But every once in a while, someone is kicked out.

When people leave, they throw a party,
Then they walk away,
Hoping to never come back to Chemo Town.

Some unlucky people come back.
No one welcomes them because
No one wants them to have to be
In Chemo Town.

### I never tell a lie

*(to the tune of "I've Got No Strings" from* Pinocchio*)*

I have these strings
That weigh me down
I can't have fun
When they're around
Through my chest
As you can see
I've got these strings on me

Uh-oh the che-emo
That's the only thing I know
I might not let it show
But it really bothers me

I have these strings
That pump me up
I can't get up
'Til that bell rings
I hate these strings
But you can see
I've got these strings on me

## *seasons*

Seasons are weird with cancer.
You have to be more careful around everything,
As if you are made of glass and the smallest exposure to something
Could make you crack.

Spring is weird with cancer.
You aren't allowed to get down in the dirt,
You should stay away from cleaning and dust.
You can't plant flowers, or even have them in your room.

Summer is weird with cancer.
You don't feel like biking or hiking,
You can't bask in the sun because of your sensitive skin,
You don't want to go outside because you are too tired.

Fall is weird with cancer.
You're not supposed to jump in leaf piles,
You are too tired to carve pumpkins,
You don't feel hungry enough to eat Thanksgiving meals.

Winter is weird with cancer.
You have to be careful not to slip or fall,
You have to avoid the flu and colds like the plague,
Your mouth feels too thick for hot chocolate.

The world spins around the way it always does,
But some things are wrong; they don't feel the same.
Feeling sick takes the fun out of the holidays.
Seasons are weird with cancer.

*in chains*

I've got these cuffs
'Round my wrists
That confine me.
They burn as they turn,
Oh, what did I do to earn
These cuffs 'round my wrists that confine me?

I've got this rope
'Round my throat
That restrains me.
It keeps me locked up tight to this bed.
It hurts in my brain and
It's driving me insane,
This rope 'round my throat that restrains me.

I've got this voice
In my ears
That abuses me.
A thought that annoys and torments.
It's keeping me in chains
And I can't avoid the pains
From the voice in my ears that abuses me.

# *therapy*

I can't talk to my therapist anymore because nothing she says can make me better.

She doesn't know the statistics.

She can't tell me I won't die.

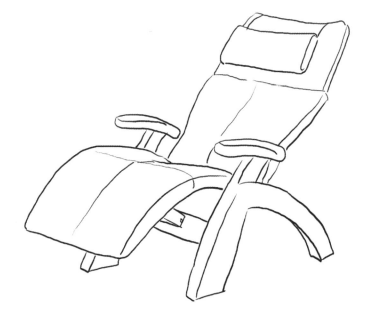

# *Imagine*

*(to the tune of "Imagine" by John Lennon)*

Imagine there's no cancer
It's kind of hard to do
No need for stress or chemo
And no transfusions, too

Imagine all the children
Growing up in peace
Yeah

Imagine there's no sickness
I wonder if I can
Nothing to change my future
No need to hold my hand

Oh, imagine all the parents
Living without fear
You

You may say I'm a dreamer
And I know there won't be ease
But I hope someday there might be
And the world will live in peace

We live in peace

Imagine there's no conflict
Now, wouldn't that be great
And everyone has healthcare
No one would have to wait

Oh, imagine all the people
Living 'cause they do
You

You may say I'm a dreamer
But I know I'm not alone
I hope someday we'll cure us
And healthy is all we've known.

## *balance*

It's hard to find your balance
When your world is so off-track
Between the good days, sad and bad,
The lightness and the black.

It's hard to remember to balance
Your hard times and your joy
When things are rough and you've had enough,
To know what to employ.

It's hard to be in balance
In a life that's ever-changing
You think you're done or that you've won
But it's always rearranging.

I sometimes forget that balance
Is something that I need
To stand upright there must be a night
With good days not guaranteed.

# *multiverse me*

I've read about the multiverse,
With worlds both old and new
With some that might even be worse
Than this trial that I'm going through.

But maybe in one I'm six feet tall
With hair and beard of white,
Where I live inside a waterfall,
And everything just feels right.

Maybe in one I live on the moon
With a purple axolotl,
And I live inside a big balloon
Where life won't go full throttle.

And maybe there's one where She didn't come back,
And I just lived normally,
And didn't know what I could lack;
I only felt light and free.

And maybe there's one when She didn't come at all,
And I had hair to spare,
And I never took that fateful fall
Or had to think about how life ain't fair.

And maybe there's one without anything bad
No sickness, pains or cries
No thinking about the lives we had
No need to say goodbyes.

In some world, I know I'm happy
Everyday, not just Week Four
And I live without feeling crappy
'Cause I know that there will be more.

## *a good place*

I know there is a good place
Whether up high or down low
A place with blue skies and sunshine
Where warm, soft breezes blow.

Where cancer never touches us
And kids are free to grow
And play amongst the daffodils
While warm, soft breezes blow.

Where one can read a book in bed
'Cause the hours go by slow
And there's always fresh-made lemonade
Where the warm, soft breezes blow.

And I know it's so much nicer there,
With all ducklings in a row
But for now, I'll sit here in this chair
While the warm, soft breezes blow.

### *Dandelion Head*

*(to be played/sung in the style of Cavetown or Peter McPoland)*

Dandelion Head
She can't keep her hair on
Her face shows the scars
Of the wear and the tear on
The lines and the cuts, they show that it's real
Oh-oh, Dandelion Head
She can't help but feel.

Dandelion Head
Her hair floats away
With the smallest of breezes
But she wishes it would stay
Puffs fly away over the cold mountain stream
Oh-oh, Dandelion Head
Life is but a dream.

Dandelion Head
She mourns for her loss
Of her now empty head
And the bridges she must cross
Dear Dandelion, if only you could see
The end of the tunnel,
That's when you'll be free.

## *Senior Speech, ver. 1*

Hi my name is Sierra Shuck-Sparer. Three years ago, I was diagnosed with high-risk medulloblastoma, a type of brain cancer. I had 30 days of radiation followed by seven months of chemotherapy. I had so much support from the teachers and students of West and from the people in my neighborhood and my community. For that, I want to say thank you. I've learned a lot about kindness, good humor, and adaptation. But I've also learned that y'all need to give yourselves the same level of care that you gave me. One of the most common things I've heard from people who mean well is "I have [fill in the blank] going on, but it's not as bad as, you know, brain cancer. You have it worse." Is that supposed to make me feel better, like "yeah, my cancer is superior to your [fill in the blank]." Ok, I know cancer is pretty bad. But [fill in the blank] sounds pretty terrible too. What I'm trying to say is, don't compare your issues with others'. It'll probably make you both feel bad. You feel bad that I feel bad, and I feel bad that you feel bad but you say you can't feel bad because I feel bad. See the problems there? It's a cycle of people feeling bad without realizing that it is ok for them to feel that way. It is ok for you to have a really bad day. Your bad day is separate from my cancer. Both suck, both come from the same pain receptors, but they are two different things, each deserving of attention and care. So, don't shortchange your problems. Instead, try to recognize that you feel terrible, and think about what would make you feel better. It's not a competition to see who has the most tragic backstory. Just think, right now, of everything you've accomplished. Every problem you've solved, success you've achieved, good grade you've made, wall you've climbed, friend you've met, story you've lived. You're about to graduate high school! And I think that's pretty amazing.

## *Senior Speech, ver. 2*

This year has been crazy. Two important things happened, one amazingly good and one amazingly terrible. One, I got to be a cast member of this year's production of *Bright Star*, which I hope you guys saw because it was absolutely incredible to be a part of. Two, I was diagnosed with a medulloblastoma relapse. Sophomore year, I was diagnosed with high-risk medulloblastoma, a type of brain cancer. I went through radiation and chemotherapy and essentially lost an entire year of school and social life while I was beating cancer. This year, I thought I was done. When I learned that Gertrude (which is what I named my tumor) had come back, I was disappointed (to put it lightly). I found out that she was back three weeks before I was supposed to perform *Bright Star*. Suddenly, all of the lyrics were put into perspective. "I have learned the brightest day can turn into the darkest night." This show, which before had just been a fun new experience, became both a physicalized version of my anxieties and distress and a beacon of hope that everything will turn out alright. "Bright star, keep shining for me. Shine on, and see me through." Right after *Bright Star* ended, I began chemo again. I had bad days, I had ok days. I was able to go to prom, and I am able to be here today. I am going to Georgia Tech next year to pursue a career in healthcare public policy. "Bright Star, keep shining for me. And one day, I'll shine for you."

## Break (2)

*August 2021 – January 2022*
*first semester of freshman year of college*

My oncologist was on the fence about whether I should do four rounds of chemo or six. My body wasn't taking the chemo very well, but it was still feasible I could do six. However, this would mean starting my first semester at Georgia Tech late, if at all. I *really* didn't want to do that. So, I only did four rounds of chemo the summer before I started school. This meant that I had the entire fall semester to recover and dive into everything college. It was wonderful.

# *choice*

Looking into the unknown
Is always difficult

To understand the enormity of a decision
Is often improbable

To know that there is no data
No real answer
(No easy one at least)
Is soul clenching
Heart-wrenching

And yet

I guess there is some part of me
That understands it

Choosing between four and six
Feeling sick or kind of better
A slightly smaller percentage
Something maybe less inevitable
A chalky pill to swallow
An upward hill to climb

The choice is never
(Will never)
Be easy

I'll have to keep choosing
What I think will let me
Keep choosing
Keep going
Keep living

Because I want to live

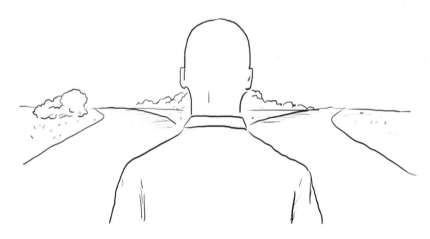

### *summary in poetry*

One morning, no doubt
You've heard all about,
I fell jumping on ice.
My flip-turns grew dizzy,
Math class in a tizzy,
Sophomore year paid the price.

The afternoon of,
Sun shining above,
I took my PSAT.
Next an MRI
(And contrast—oh my!)
Revealed an evil entity.

I screamed, I cried,
"Who let you inside?"
But no one answered me.
The robbers instead
Just entered my head
Through the top balcony.

To Memphis we drove,
And thank whatever's above,
The best neurosurgeon was in.
Then about one week later,
I have a six-inch crater,
And doctor appointments—a dozen.

The first thing I needed
(And port placement succeeded)
Was radiation: craniospinal.
I got a mask of green
And a Darth Vader theme
Until I reached 30—the final.

The next thing I got
Was chemical rot;
Seven months I endured.
There were good and bad days,
But I just had to stay
Because in August I was then cured.

Junior year
Filled with cheer
As I returned to school.
The classes were hard
But we didn't get far;
We followed COVID-19's rule.

The summer after
Was filled with laughter
As I decided to build up my strength.
I was swimming again,
Even making more friends
Finding and riding the wavelength.

Senior year
I knew I'd appear
With the wisdom of what I learned,
But who'd have thunk
That with God-awful funk
Gertrude had again returned.

Cycle 1: a doozy
Cycle 2: so woozy
Plus graduation and prom in between.
Cycle 3: a fight
Cycle 4: just might
Be the end of my whole college dream.

All that they said
Was they didn't know ahead
If she'll come back to haunt once more
The decision was mine
With limited time
So I decided to block out the tumor.

A good choice? I just heard the voice,
Crying out into the night: "Live, live, live!"
I might.

## *journal 7-8-21*

I wonder what is beyond.

Is it a Good and Bad place? Is it a judgement of my actions on a holy or unholy spectrum? Will I be punished for believing that there is no beyond?

Maybe there will be a library where I will have the opportunity to correct my regrets.
Maybe there will be a glowing pathway into the next stage of existence.
Maybe I will be recycled into a new life form, merging back into the circle of life.
Maybe there is nothing.

I hate to think there is nothing. I mean, it makes sense, given the vastness of the universe, that there can't possibly be enough room to fit every living soul that ever existed over seven billion years. But, I still feel significant, despite what I should believe. Maybe it helps me go on. Who knows.

I understand the want for salvation. The idea that, if you believe in a faith so much, it will take you to a better place. That, when everyone else falls to a miserable, faithless demise, you will be okay. I do believe that faith is a good thing. Faith and hope and charity equals three (and that's a magic number). It is good to have faith in each other and in humankind.

I read a book once, called *Elsewhere* by Gabrielle Zevin. It is my favorite idea for what is beyond. In *Elsewhere*, the place where people arrive once they have passed away, the citizens age backwards, until they are returned to Earth as babies, their essences still intact. Also, while they are in Elsewhere, they can watch their living friends and families (although this can become a bad obsession). It is a very good book. I recommend it.

I want to believe I can exist when I'm gone. I want you to believe it too. I want you to know that I'll be with you. It's okay. It'll be okay.

## hugging sideways

Gertrude changed my life in many ways,
Both big and small.

She made me lose
My love of skating,
My speed in swimming,
My endurance in everything.

She made me lose
My muscles and breath
My balance and stability
My hearing and voice.

She made me lose
Three-fourths of my sophomore year,
The beginning of my junior year,
The end of my senior year.

But what hurts the most,
On days when I'm feeling alright,
Is the realization that I twist when I hug,
Guarding the right side of my body
From human contact.

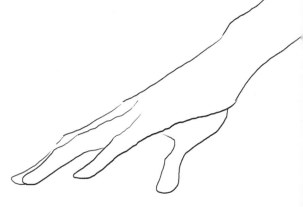

This is because of my port,
A reminder of being sick,
Why my arm doesn't swing
When I walk.

And then knowing that there is
A side of me that will never heal,
That will always be wary of being
Too close.

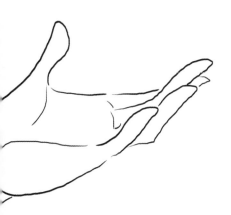

## *eyelashes pt. 3*

Every once in a while,
My eyelashes fall out again,
For absolutely no reason.
Even though it's been months since
My treatment stopped,
And my hair grew back,
And I forget about fearing.

They get into my eyes again.
Usually easy to remove, but sometimes
A light-colored eyelash hides in
The corners of my eye
And makes it water.

I pull out the loose ones
(Which at this point, is most)
And then I'm left with the reminder
That I am sick.

Yes they'll grow back,
But never completely.

### Don't think hard, it's alright

*(to the tune of "Don't Think Twice, It's All Right" by Bob Dylan)*

Now it ain't no use to sit and wonder why, girl
Since we don't know anyhow
And it ain't no use to just sit there and cry, girl
What good will it do right now?

When the tumor stays after every round
I just wanna collapse here on the ground
But I know there's no help in just laying around
So don't think too hard, it's alright

Now it ain't no use in telling me I'm brave, girl
I know but I don't believe
And it ain't no use in cutting off my strings, girl
I don't think I'll ever truly be free

Still I wish there was something I could think or know
That would let me see next Christmas snow
I'm scared to death but I won't let it show
But don't think too hard, it's alright

It ain't no use in worrying about the pause, girl
If you just take your time
And it ain't no use in focusing on the loss, girl
If you just feel the rhythm and the rhyme

I'm just thinking about the many times we had
The good, the medium, and the bad
The times when I almost drowned in the deepening sad
But don't think too hard, I'll be alright

# *Pro Tips for Going Through Cancer Treatment (legit, no joke)*

1. For proton radiation, you cannot move if you are not sedated. If you move, they have to start over.
    a. You can listen to podcasts or music while having radiation, but know that the radiation techs can hear it too, so don't play something like "More Than Survive" from *Be More Chill* unless you want to hear your radiation techs laughing at the line "I'm waiting for my porno to load" (as a random, non-specific example).
2. When experiencing cranio-radiation (head/brain radiation), you may experience a weird smell/sensation. Counteract this by asking the radiation tech to put a scented cloth under your nose before treatment starts.
    a. Probably don't change smells if they clash with each other. The smells will stick to the mask, so you may be left with something that smells like watermelon mint (again, as a random, non-specific example).
3. When lying on a metal radiation table, your butt may start to hurt after 1 or 1.5 hours. This pain can be directed towards stress balls.
    a. I recommend foam stress balls. You can tear these apart in one hand and it is very satisfying. I do not recommend the ones with gel inside because if you tear them open you will have gel on your hands and it will feel and smell gross.
4. As soon as your hair starts falling out in big chunks, you should shave it off, unless you have a broom, a working vacuum, a lint roller, and are ok with hair everywhere.
    a. You can use a lint roller to no-razor-shave your hair (if it's short enough, or if it's just stubble) with a 75% success rate.
5. Let the doctors/nurses know everything you feel. It's all important.
    a. If you get a small "mosquito bite" after a blood/platelet transfusion (or any other medicine infusion), call and tell a nurse. This could be the start of an allergic reaction (mine led to an anaphylactic reaction, but I was able to be ok because I told my nurse as soon as I noticed it).
6. You may encounter some sub-par nurses. They are rare, but they sometimes occur.
    a. I call them "Susans" (say "Susan" like how Bob says it in *Monsters vs. Aliens*)
    b. Don't be mean to them but maybe ask for someone else in the future…
7. Always ask for the hospital therapy animals.
    a. If you're at East Tennessee Children's Hospital on a Friday, ask for Rudy. He is great.
8. Eat ANYTHING. The higher the carbs, the better.

    a.   If you find yourself eating increasingly fewer portions of food, try doing little snacks throughout the day instead of a lot of food three times per day.

    b.   If you crave a milkshake, drink it.

9.   If Ensure protein drinks do not taste good to you (this is ok; they are gross), you can try Carnation Instant Breakfast drinks, which can be mixed into milkshakes or smoothies.

10.  Before getting an IV, drink lots of water, and put a hot pad on the area you are getting accessed by (ask for these). This will ensure your veins can be easily accessed and you don't have to get stuck multiple times until your nurse can find a good vein.

    a.   Additionally, you can use numbing cream to help with surface pain.

11.  Wheelchairs are fun if you can drive yourself, but it's also nice when people push you.

    a.   You can hang backpacks on the backs of wheelchairs, or push them with your backpack in the seat.

    b.   Wagons are also helpful to hold stuff and small kids.

12.  Always have a go-bag ready for emergency snacks, thermometers and medicine, hygiene stuff, fuzzy socks, extra PJs, water/Sprite, etc.

    a.   This is helpful for late-night panic trips to the Med Room.

13.  Don't say "I need hats and fuzzy socks" to friends and family, even though you will need hats and fuzzy socks. You don't need to be overwhelmed by hats and fuzzy socks.

    a.   Make an Amazon Wish List so people can know specifically what you might like.

14.  You will receive large amounts of coloring books (mostly adult) from well-meaning people. These can be donated to people who have the time/patience to finish them.

    a.   See above.

15.  It's ok to have bad days. Try not to take it out on the hospital staff.

16.  Go easy on yourself. Don't let yourself be rushed into something that you're not ready for.

17.  It's ok to pause social media activity, leave messages unread, or leave mail unopened. Take your time.

18.  It will probably be frustrating to transition from treatment to life, but know there will always be people who support and love you and who will help you find your footing and grow stronger.

19.  Therapists can be helpful for a non-family/friend person to vent to.

20.  Art therapy is very helpful (for me; find what works best for you).

21.  There are so many people who love you and are cheering you on. They will support you no matter what happens. You got this.

# A head of hair

*(sung with a ukulele accompaniment, in the style of Grace VanderWaal)*

I look around
Each and every day
I try to stay cool
But something gets in my way

And life is so unfair
'Cause all I really wish for is a full head of hair

That's really all I need
All I really need is a full head of hair

Frizzy or curly, it gets in my face,
Long and blonde and just so out of place,
Brown and straight and even redheads too
All I really want is to look like you

Pigtails or bobs or maybe just some braids
A bun or headband is all it would take
For me to feel like I don't need a hat
Oh, I wish I looked just like that

And life is so unfair
'Cause all I really want is a full head of hair

'Cause it would mean I made it through
And it would mean that I was done with you
And I would feel just so alive
No need to cover up the scars and hide

No need to hide

And even though
I've had to go
Through many rounds
Of chemo

I still will share
My worst despair
Is how I only wish
For a full head of hair

## *cotton candy thoughts*

I notice sometimes,
When I am writing an essay or a memo,
When I am participating in a discussion,
When I am having a normal conversation,
That the words I am looking for
Float             away             just             out             of             reach.

Struggling to piece them together.
How do I articulate?
Stringing sugary syllables around a rod of coherency.

I guess it happens quickly,
But in my mind, it feels like forever.
As I am                                    stranded,
Grasping at the wisps
Of colored crystals
As they expand, thicken, change
Into what I want to say.

It is not easy.
Do I make it look easy?
Years of practice,
Learning how to spin without getting dizzy.
But sometimes I still get                       lost,
Losing my words to a bottle of pills.

So some days I sit staring off into space
Gathering my thoughts like cotton candy.

## *my eyebrows*

I started doing my eyebrows in middle school.
They were uneven and lopsided.
I never wore makeup or anything, just plucked my eyebrows.

I have always been self-conscious about them.
Or at least I was, until they fell out.
Then I had no eyebrows to worry about.

When they grew back, I controlled the shape.
They looked, in my eyes, good.
I got compliments on my eyebrows.

They became something I was proud of.
Something good that came of my seven months of chemo:
My eyebrows!

Then, of course, my cancer returned.
My eyebrows fell out.
Like everything I had finally gotten back after my treatment, they were gone.

Now, after four more months of chemo, they're back.
They are sometimes patchy, sometimes fine.
They are light (but not blonde), dark (but not brown).

They are not perfect.
But I think that's ok.
I just don't want to lose them again.

## high school

We were talking about high school and I didn't know what to say because my high school experience was mostly cancer. I only went to school for about 2.5 years total.

- 1 freshman year
- 0.25 sophomore year (cancer)
- 0.5 junior year (between cancer and COVID)
- 0.75 senior year (cancer)

So, yeah. I have a lot to talk about, but not much of it is about high school, and most of it makes people uncomfortable.

*Sometimes I get nostalgic for things that are still here.*
*I guess I'm just imagining having to leave.*

## Maurice Sendak

Once, in an interview, he said:
"I'm finding out as I'm aging that I'm in love with the world."

I heard this quote and I wrote it down,
Thinking about it as I lie in bed
Staring up at the ceiling.

I think of it as I walk through the Georgia Tech campus,
Inhaling the sweet smell of Gingko trees,
Carrying my food truck fusion,
Watching the sun set over the Atlanta buildings.

I think of it when I hold my cat, Tiger,
Kissing her head and rubbing her paws,
As I sit in the green chair in my living room,
Looking out the window at the falling snow.

I think of it when I see something
So unique, so strange
That only one person in the entire world
Thought of it and made it real.

Whenever I am having a bad day,
When I can only look at the ground and not the flowers or the sky,
When the shades of green in the trees blur together,
When I think about not being able to come back here,
I close my eyes.
And I breathe.

I am in love with this world.

# Third

*January 2022 – May 2022*
*second semester of freshman year of college*

Even though it was expected, I was still pretty disappointed when my oncologist told me I relapsed again. Dang it. The chemo was supposed to be "mild." My oncologist said one doctor has "had a patient on it for years" (very reassuring). So, I decided to do chemo in Knoxville, going home from Georgia Tech every Thursday night after my last class and doing chemo on the next Friday (because I had no Friday classes). Then I would stay home and recover on Saturday, then be driven back to Atlanta on Sunday. I would rest in my dorm, doing classes virtually on Monday and Tuesday before going back on Wednesday. It was rough. But I loved GT too much to stop. Also, I got into the summer 2022 Oxford study abroad program and my oncologist said I could stop chemo before the trip, so I would have the entire summer to roam around Europe and feel not-crappy. All I had to do was make it through the four more months of chemo. The promise of a break and the friends I had at GT kept me going. I keep going.

### *again and again and again and again and again and again and again and again and again*

It happened again.
Why do I even try to get my hopes up?
Foolishly thinking they would let me off the hook, off the line,
That I would be free for more than one week at a time.

Because She never stops, I can never stop.
Geez, give me a break, please
I know this summer will be enough of a break for a while,
But I don't know how I can continue going
Week to week, wondering how long it will take
For me to be able to stop nausea meds,
Walk strongly up a hill without stopping,
Roll up my sleeves without fear of burning,
Open my eyes with no blurry, fuzzy feeling.

I always aim optimistically (foolishly)
For the lowest number they give me,
But then I forget the high-end number,
So it always surprises me when I have to do
That high-end number.

From three to four,
Four to six,
A little to a lot,
More weeks left to lay
In the bed I never made
Sleeping with coins on my eyes
In payment to Her,
Giving Her all of my strength,
Weight, agility, motivation.

"Third time's the charm."
I sure hope so,
But my oncologist hinted that I might have
More after the summer.
Is this included in the "third time"
Or did I miss the luck?
Again and again and again.

## I guess it's happening again

I guess it's happening again
The time of year, always when
I'm settling in, I'm moving on
I've found new joy and a new way to look upon
The world as it watches in the indifferent way of fate.

So I guess I'll have to relearn how to go down stairs
And I guess I'll have to hug different 'cause my port is still in there
And I guess I'll have to (once again) say goodbye to my hair

And goodbye to the people I've come to know
And goodbye to the amount of room I've had to grow
And goodbye to the schoolwork I love and hate
And goodbye to the good food that I once ate
And goodbye to the dorm rooms and study halls
And goodbye, goodbye, goodbye.

## *what it feels like*

(*sung with piano*)

When you think you've won the prize but it's somebody else,
When you barely can't reach the highest place on your shelf,
When you think you should be happy but you're just not yourself,
That is how it feels.

When you walk into a room and forget what for,
When you accidentally shut your coat in a door
And then right outside it suddenly starts to pour,
That is how it feels.

When you think it will be cold outdoors but it's really not,
When you think the stove is off but it is still hot,
When you think you know the answer but you straight-up forgot,
That is how it feels.

When you look over a high cliff and your stomach's churning,
When you ate too much hot food and your mouth is burning,
When you think the ride is done but it is still turning,
That is how it feels.

Dizzy and disorienting and just plain wack,
You think you're going forward but you're two steps back,
You think you've got it all but realize what you lack,
And you knock over the paper that you put in a stack,
And your light goes off when reading so you're left in the black,
And you didn't bring food with you but you want a snack,
And every single train of thought is running off its track,

That is how it feels.

### *when will I get better?*

I always wonder when I will get better.
Today or tomorrow or next week or next year?

Sometimes I think that
Every time I feel like I'm better,
Every time I think I'm getting stronger,
My body rebels and
She returns.

Living is sometimes heavy when
I think that
Killing her is so hard to do but I'm stuck until we can,
Evermore stuck in this loop of better and worse and better again.

Now I feel more hope because
Everyone acts like I am free from the
Vise of her and treatment. Am I?
Encouragements help to a certain extent but
Really, when will I get better?

## Hey St. Jude

*(to the tune "Hey Jude" by The Beatles)*

Hey St. Jude,
Don't let me down.
Take my cancer
And make me better.
Remember, I'm only 18 years old,
I have yet to start my life ahead.

Hey St. Jude,
I won't be afraid
Just as long as
You help me out here
Remember, I've so much I want to do,
I have yet to go to Europe this summer.

Don't you know I can't let her win
Hey St. Jude, begin
Another round of chemo
And then done.

Please no more chemo, no no no no.

Hey St. Jude,
Please be my friend
Get rid of Gertrude
Now and forever.
Remember, I want to live a full life
So show me how dark
Can get lighter.

## *remember me*

I hope you remember me,
The person I was before everything started,
And, even, the person I was at my best.

Remember how I could ice skate so well?
How my legs were strong and my head was clear.
I was good.
I didn't get dizzy when I spun.
I could skate for hours without feeling tired,
Remember how I could jump so high and never lose my balance.

Remember how I could swim?
I was strong and my back was wide.
I was good.
I dropped over a second every year.
My first 500 freestyle, I won.
The summer before she came, I finally got 27.99 seconds for my 50 free.
Remember that my butterfly was beautiful.

Remember when I started rock climbing?
I loved the calluses on my hands.
My wide shoulders and strong legs helped me fly up the wall,
My endurance let us climb 600 feet in Yosemite.
Remember how I was just getting started.

Remember when I could climb trees,
Skip down stairs,
Heal from cuts,
Ride a bike,
Go on hikes,
Play piano (Why is that gone? It shouldn't be.)

Just remember me please.

Remember how I could laugh?
Without a weight on my chest or a hole in my stomach,
When my heart wasn't heavy and my throat wasn't thick,
And I could take medication without feeling sick,

Please remember me.

Sometimes I forget.
Sometimes I remember, and it hurts.
Sometimes I know what I have.
But it's hard.
So please, for me, remember.

## *cancer playlist pt. 1: songs for when I want to feel sad*

"If You Knew My Story" from *Bright Star*
"Not Today" by Alessia Cara
"Gotta Be a Reason" by Alec Benjamin
"Night Changes" by One Direction
"Part of Your World" from *The Little Mermaid*
"Because of You" by Kelly Clarkson
"Reflection" from *Mulan*
"idontwannabeyouanymore" by Billie Eilish
"Lion's Den" by Grace VanderWaal
"She Used to Be Mine" by Sarah Bareilles
"Let Her Go" by Passenger
"Talking to the Moon" by Bruno Mars
"lovely" by Billie Eilish & Khalid
"This is Home" by Cavetown
"Cancer" by twenty one pilots
"Exhausted" by chloe moriondo
"Death Bed (Coffee for Your Head)" by Powfu

*I want to put enough of myself into the world so that when I'm gone, you'll remember me.*

## I don't know if I can do this

Whispers sowing doubt.
Seeds growing under the dark skies.
Flower blooming into rot.
Decay soaked in the roots.
Birth of new whispers.

### *cancer playlist pt. 2: songs for when I want to feel angry (and sad)*

"Jealous" by Labrinth

"Heart of Stone" from *SIX*

"Sign of the Times" by Harry Styles

"Happier Than Ever" by Billie Eilish

"Breathe" from *In the Heights*

"Waving Through a Window" from *Dear Evan Hansen*

"Numb Little Bug" by Em Beihold

"jealousy, jealousy" by Olivia Rodrigo

"Born Without a Heart" by Faouzia

"brutal" by Olivia Rodrigo

"Surface Pressure" from *Encanto*

"good 4 u" by Olivia Rodrigo

"Let Me Be Happy" by SM6

"Wake Me When It's Over" by Faouzia

"As It Was" by Harry Styles

"Wake Me Up" by Avicii

"Better Days" by OneRepublic

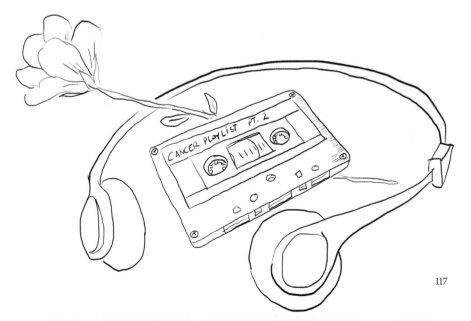

## to Gertrude

I'd write you some hate mail
If you knew how to read
I'd burn down your house
If you owned the deed
I'd take everything
You want or you need
So hopefully someday I'd finally be freed.

If I was your lifeguard
I'd make sure you drown
If you want to go up
I'd pull you way down
If you tried to smile
I'd turn it into a frown
I hate to be cruel, but you need to leave town.

I hate all your friends
And your humor is wack
If I find a blade
I'll stab you in the back
You won't let me breathe,
Won't cut me some slack
There's so much I hate about your silly act.

Don't you know that I hate to be mean
But you started this; you caused a scene
Couldn't leave me alone when I was fifteen
Come out of the shadows, you cowardly fiend.

# *wonder*

Have you ever wondered what it's like to be sick?
To have everything you know thrown out the window,
To have your strength sapped through your veins,
To not be hungry,
To feel weak.

I have wondered what it's like to not be sick.
To not worry about dying,
To not worry about losing out on parties and events,
To not feel like every moment can be taken from me by the drops of chemicals,
To not have to remind myself that it gets better.

Do you wonder how I feel?
Do you think about how much I lose to have one week of calm?

Do you wonder why I am happy when I see you?
It's because I know I might not again.
Do you wonder why I stop to look at all of the trees and flowers?
It's because I dread the days when all I see are flat colors.
Do you wonder why I try to do so much?
It's because I want to check as many things as I can off my bucket list.

The good days feel so good because the other days feel so bad.
I hope you wonder about me.

## *hair*

I think that people don't realize how much they value their hair,
How much their entire appearance and mental state depends on their hair.

For me, hair means that I am growing healthier, that my body is healing,
That I am done with cancer treatments and I am getting better.

I have had to look into the mirror three times now
Knowing that I am sick again.

It's always the first sight after it's been shaved off that makes me sad.
Rubbing my bald head, mourning my loss.

My dad shaved it off the first two times.
I had to go to a Super Cuts in Atlanta by myself for the third.

When your hair starts falling out, it's weird; it's not supposed to happen.
A healthy person has healthy hair. An unhealthy person has no hair.

You run your fingers through your hair and pull away with some between your fingers.
You didn't even feel the roots part from your head.

The razor feels cold against my skin.
It is no guard, to make my cleanup easier.

Sometimes I take a lint roller and go back over so I don't leave any bits on my pillow.
It comes right off, as if it is dust.

Somedays I feel like I am dust,
Fighting against the wind to stay where I am.

## *Super Cuts*

When I went to the Super Cuts, it was a Wednesday.
My philosophy class was canceled, so I only had my 8:00 a.m. English.
My hair started falling out the night before.
I had a whole day ahead of me.
I walked to the Super Cuts.

It was warm; the high was close to 80 degrees, in February.
But it poured.
The sky was cloudy and the air was thick.
My umbrella fought to stay upright against the wind.
I had to walk through a fraternity's yard to avoid the puddles.

The first daffodils popped up last weekend.
Their yellow petals stood out against the gray day.
Their heads drooped over their stems, weighed down by the dew and water droplets.
They watched me as I passed, and their heads sank lower.
Yellow is supposed to be happy, but I just felt sick.

When I reached the salon, there was only one person working.
She was very nice. Quiet. Sometimes I couldn't hear her.
The salon was playing "Shake It Off" by Taylor Swift.
I sat in the chair and stared at my feet, at my soggy shoes and socks.
My hair came out in clumps as the razor buzzed.

I didn't look into the mirror. I didn't want to cry there.
I think she said, "I'm sorry." I don't remember.
I got some food. Took a nap.
Reminded myself that I just need to make it to May.
Bought some cute hats from Amazon.

Kept going.

## the sun smiled

It's amazing
That even after everything,
Even after yesterday's gloom,
Today the sun smiled at me.

I looked up at the marble blue sky
With its fluffy splashes of clouds
And I sighed,
Thinking about how wonderful the day is.

The sun smiled as I walked through campus,
As I climbed Freshman Hill,
As I walked up the rainbow stairs,
As I breathed in the sweet smell that comes after rain.

The daffodils shone brighter today
Than I had ever seen them before.
Their faces looked up and watched me,
Smiling as we shook off the heavy winter and entered into spring.

I walked to dinner tonight
Waving to the people I knew
In the deep blue evening light
And the glow of a sun that had just set.

The stars and the city lights
Guided my way
Past the old brick dorms and the church-turned-dining hall.
I laughed at the absurdity. At the beauty.

I thought about how yesterday was so dark.
I wondered how I felt so different today.
I hope that, when I feel so awful and alone,
I remember how it feels when the sun smiles at me.

I keep going.

*I'm so thankful for the people who make the bad days worth it.*

# *cancer playlist pt. 3: songs for when I want to feel strong*

"In My Blood" by Shawn Mendes

"Champion" by Fall Out Boy

"Keep Your Head Up" by Andy Grammer

"It's OK" by Nightbirde

"I Smile" by Kirk Franklin

"Rise Up" by Andra Day

"Girl on Fire" by Alicia Keys

"Damn It Feels Good To Be Me" by Andy Grammar

"Water Me" by Lizzo

"Way Less Sad" by AJR

"Since U Been Gone" by Kelly Clarkson

"Better Get to Livin'" by Dolly Parton

"So Much More Than This" by Grace VanderWaal

"Anthem" by Walk off the Earth

"Youth" by Shawn Mendes ft. Khalid

"Scars to Your Beautiful" by Alessia Cara

"It's Time" by Imagine Dragons

"When Life Is Good Again" by Dolly Parton

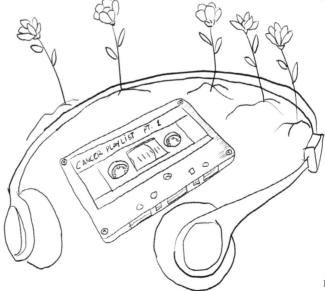

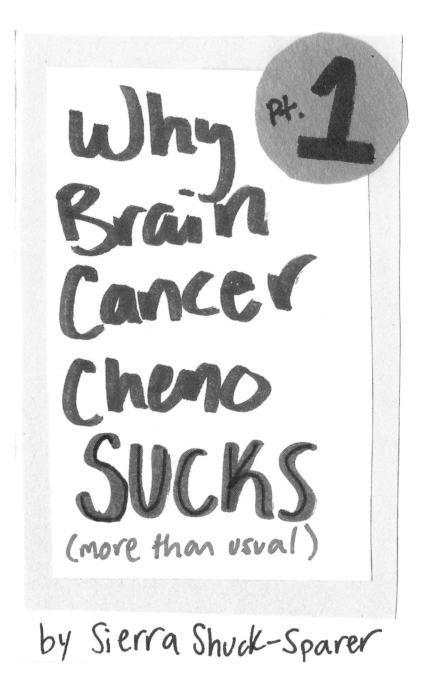

Why Brain Cancer Chemo SUCKS (more than usual) pt. 1

by Sierra Shuck-Sparer

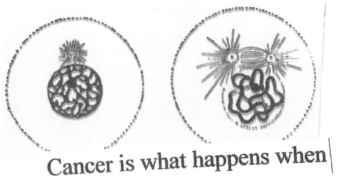

Cancer is what happens when

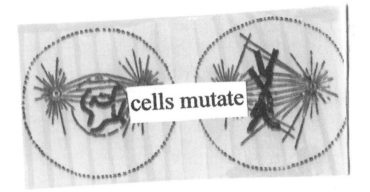

cells mutate

in bad ways.

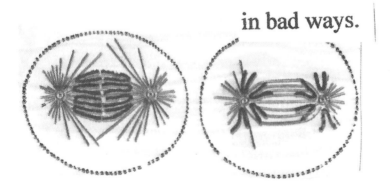

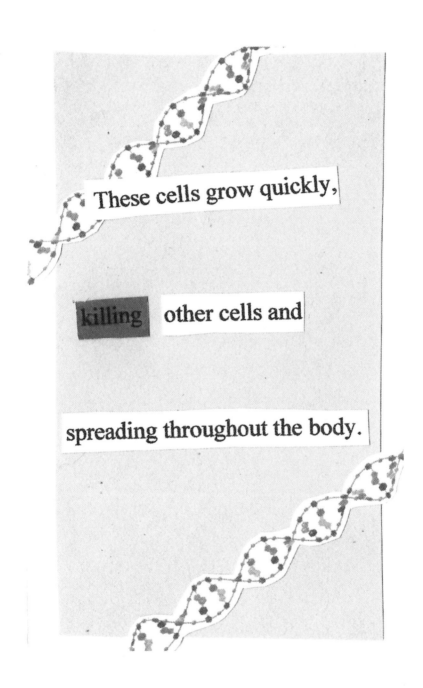

These cells grow quickly,

killing other cells and

spreading throughout the body.

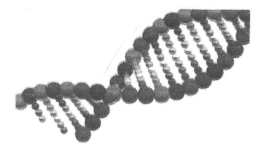

It can be in different areas of the brain

and can cause different issues.

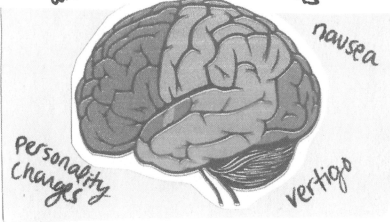

dizziness

headaches

nausea

personality changes

vertigo

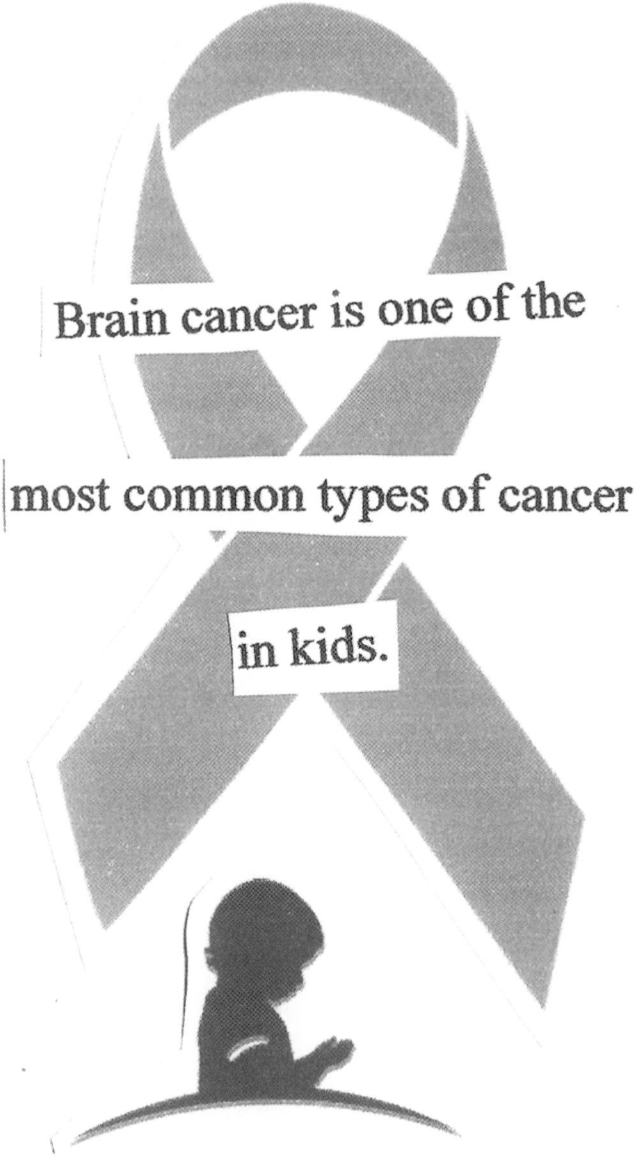

Brain cancer is one of the

most common types of cancer

in kids.

My cancer, medulloblastoma,

grows right on the brainstem,

which connects the brain to the spine.

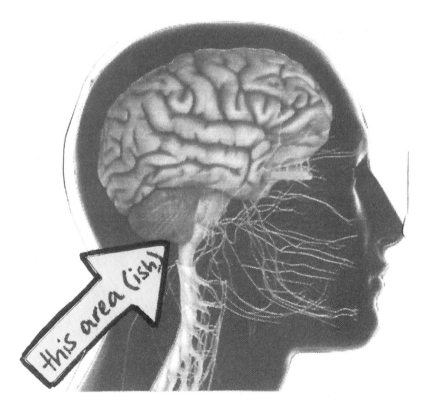

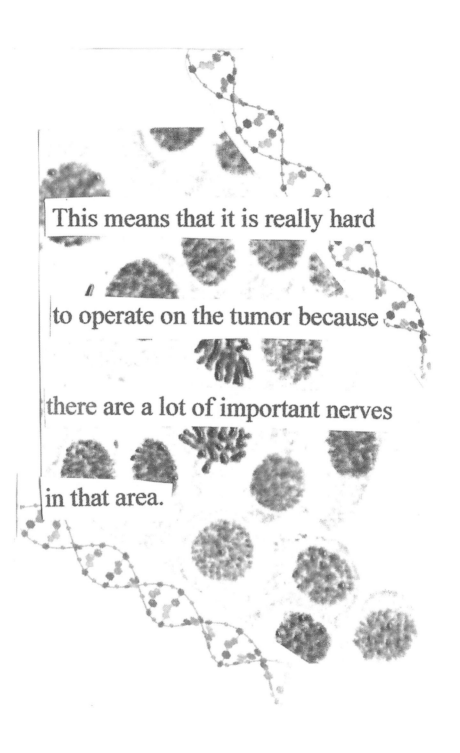

This means that it is really hard

to operate on the tumor because

there are a lot of important nerves

in that area.

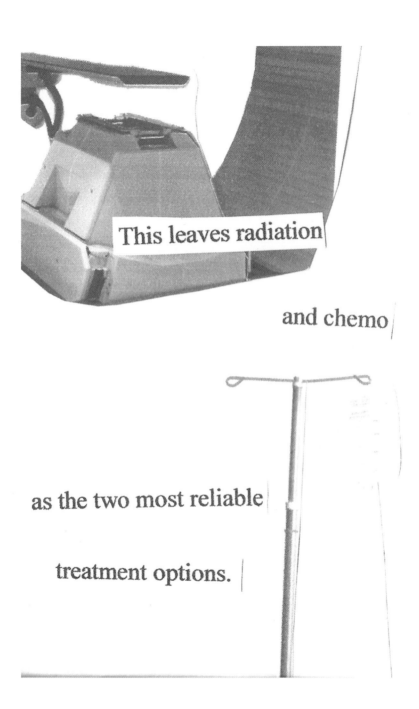

This leaves radiation

and chemo

as the two most reliable

treatment options.

# Why pt. 2 Brain Cancer Chemo SUCKS (more than usual)

by Sierra Shuck-Sparer

Chemotherapy is when oncologists

use specific chemicals to try to

kill off or reduce a cancer.

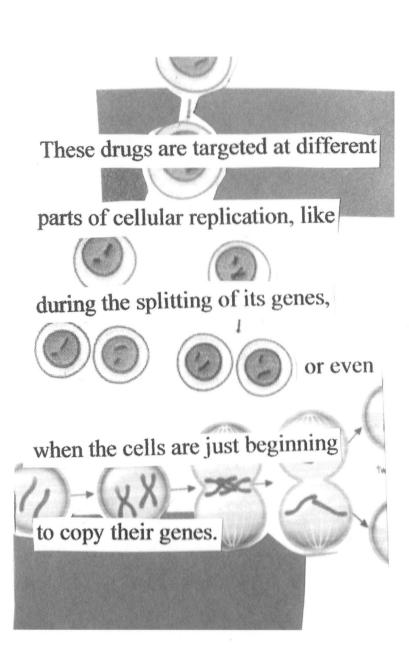

These drugs are targeted at different

parts of cellular replication, like

during the splitting of its genes,

or even

when the cells are just beginning

to copy their genes.

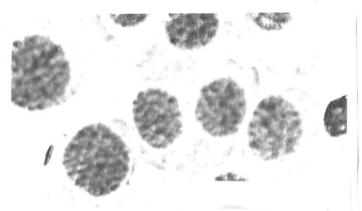

This way, the drugs will target

the quickly dividing cancer cells

and not the rest of the body.

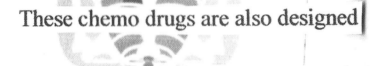

These chemo drugs are also designed

to only attack fast-replicating cells.

However some regular body cells

also divide quickly.

These include hair follicles

(which is why people who are

having chemo lose their hair),

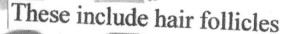

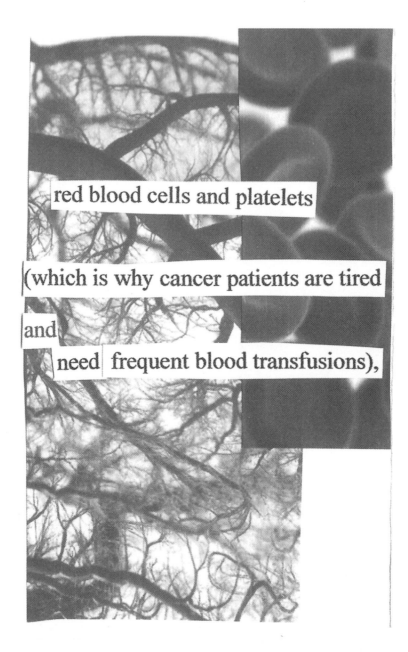

red blood cells and platelets

(which is why cancer patients are tired

and

need frequent blood transfusions),

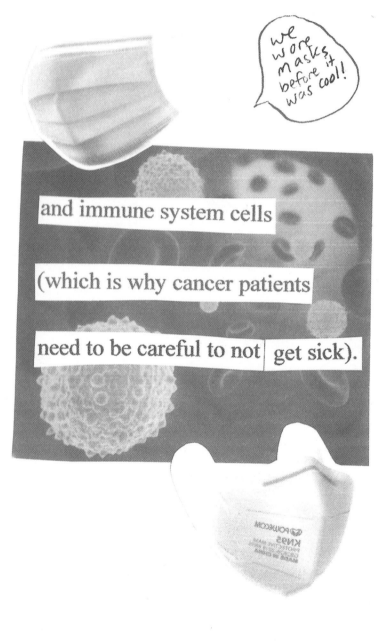

and immune system cells

(which is why cancer patients

need to be careful to not get sick).

# Why Brain Cancer Chemo SUCKS (more than usual)

Pt. 3

by Sierra Shuck-Sparer

The side effects of chemo include: *but aren't limited to)*

 vomiting,

mouth sores,

 dizziness,

weight loss, weight gain,

fatigue, rashes,

 diarrhea, constipation,

loss of appetite,

and so on.

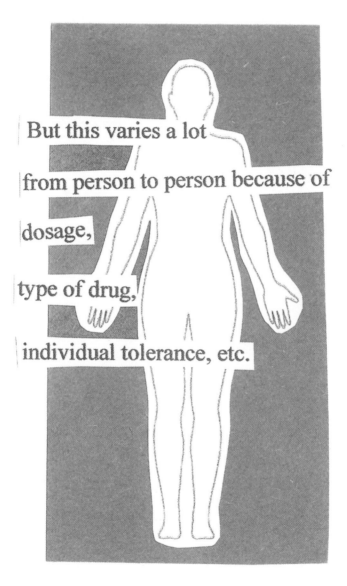

But this varies a lot from person to person because of

dosage,

type of drug,

individual tolerance, etc.

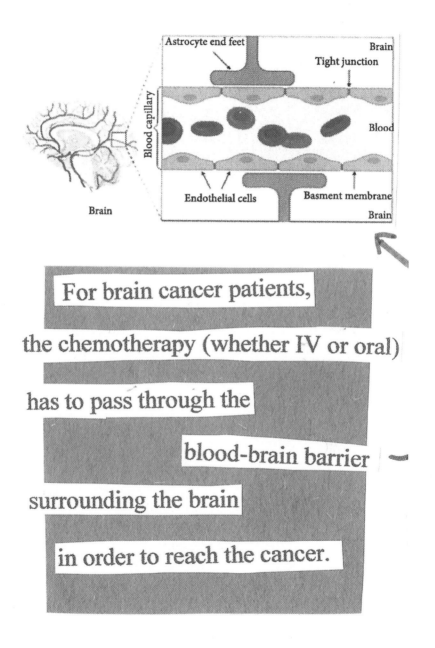

For brain cancer patients,

the chemotherapy (whether IV or oral)

has to pass through the

blood-brain barrier

surrounding the brain

in order to reach the cancer.

This means that the dosage has to be higher than for other patients, and the chemo cycles have to be longer to make sure enough chemicals enter the brain to kill the cancer inside.

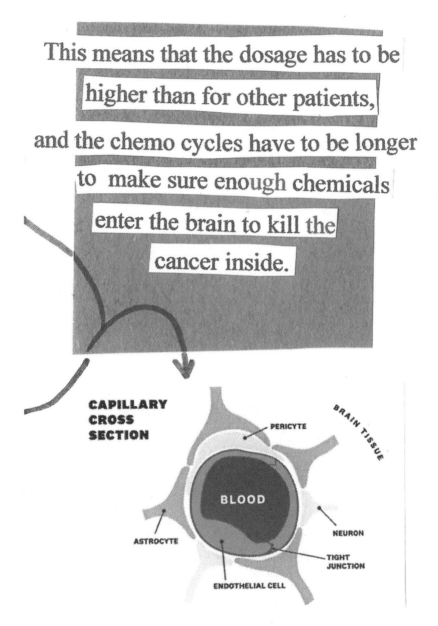

CAPILLARY CROSS SECTION

PERICYTE

BRAIN TISSUE

BLOOD

ASTROCYTE

NEURON

TIGHT JUNCTION

ENDOTHELIAL CELL

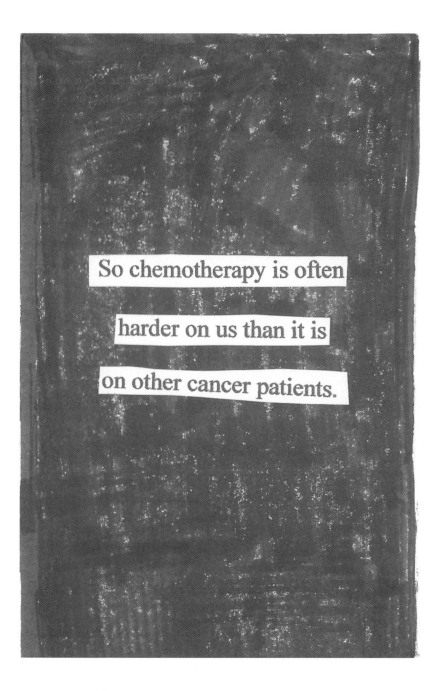

So chemotherapy is often

harder on us than it is

on other cancer patients.

This is not always true,

and it depends on what chemo it is

and who is receiving it,

but…

As a connoisseur of chemotherapy,

I can tell you that

IT SUCKS!!!

# it's 10:27 p.m. and I'm feeling depressed

It's 10:27 p.m. on a Tuesday night. I just got back from Knoxville.
This is my second-to-last treatment, and it hit really hard.
I feel so sick and tired.
I'm alone in my dorm room. Everyone is out or studying.
I popped some popcorn to share but now it's cold.
The kernels feel like Styrofoam and taste like nothing.

My room is a mess. It always is after chemo. Bags thrown everywhere.
I usually feel well enough to move them a few days after chemo. It's not time yet.
It annoys me seeing my roommate stepping over my stuff, mostly because
It's my fault it's in her way.
I realized I missed the movie watch party for my English class, even though I have been
Sitting here doing nothing ever since I got here.

I texted a friend, asked if she was at her dorm,
So I could come and sit and be sad at her place instead of mine,
But she was out, busy studying. Four more weeks left of school.
One more chemo treatment before the semester ends.
Then I get to go to Europe, and I am going to have a great time,
As long as it doesn't get canceled (the world is really messed up right now).

I know I'll feel better in a few days.
I know I'll feel better over the summer.
But my doctor said my chemo would be paused for this trip.
Meaning it will *resume* when I get back. When the next semester starts.

This is "maintenance chemo." One doctor has "had a patient on it for years."
Is that going to be me? Am I going to be strung from week to week,
Depending on what is making me feel bad to prolong how long I am going to feel bad,
With the hopes that at some point, it will miraculously reduce my cancer?

I haven't wanted to say it but I am going to say it now because I feel so depressed and
hopeless:
After a first high-risk medulloblastoma (the brain cancer that I have) relapse,
Your chance of living in the next five years is 30%.
Your chance of dying is 70%.

I increasingly feel like the odds are not in my favor, even though they never were to begin with.

*I'm not scared of dying, but I'm sad of not living.*

## *participation award*

I'm joining as many organizations as I can
So more people will remember me

I'm saying hi to more people
So they might think of me

I'm trying to tell my story
So they will understand

I regret the opportunities I've missed
To build all the bridges I can

But I am and I'll keep trying
So they might give me a participation award

*forgetting*

I forget to write something down and then it is gone, wisping away, and whispering barely out of earshot as I struggle to remember the feeling of a ghost.

## *jealous*

Of the way you run with such confidence,
Not worrying about tripping and falling.

Of the way you say "just my luck" over the smallest things,
Not knowing there are many more things that are far unluckier.

Of the way you never had to change your entire life,
Living each day with the assurance of the next being the same.

Of the way you are hungry, always looking for new foods to eat and places to go,
Without thinking about the possibility of not being able to eat or move.

Of the way you aren't expecting to die,
How you walk around without carrying the expectation of someday never coming back.

I'm jealous of the way you live.

## a good thing

Maybe it's a good thing that I won't see
The Earth overheating, the oil-full sea,
The nuclear destruction caused by World War III,
Maybe it's a good thing that I won't see.

Maybe it's a good thing that I won't feel
The lack of ozone caused by automobiles
The burning trees that will never heal
Maybe it's a good thing that I won't feel.

Maybe it's a good thing that I won't know
A world run by dictator overthrow
Without any joy or even snow
Maybe it's a good thing that I won't know.

But how can it be good when I'll never see
My cousins' weddings, my grandkids' glee
My brother getting his college degree
Oh, I really do want to see.

And how can it be good if I never feel
The soft cat fur, the love that is real
The shuffle of playing cards, getting to deal
Oh, I really do want to feel.

How could it be good if I never know
How the people around me learn and grow
My jealousy gone with my sorrow.
How can it be good if I never know?

*Crying [usually] makes me feel better.*

## Quotes from Margaret Edson's play Wit *that I deeply connect to*

*(all from Vivian, who is undergoing ovarian cancer treatment)*

[*when people ask, "how do you feel?"*]
"I just say, 'Fine.'
Of course it is not very often that I do feel fine.
I have been asked 'How are you feeling today?' while I was throwing up into a plastic washbasin. I have been asked as I was emerging from a four-hour operation with a tube in every orifice, 'How are you feeling today?'
I am waiting for the moment when someone asks me this question and I am dead.
I'm a little sorry I'll miss that." p. 14

"One thing can be said for an eight-month course of cancer treatment: it is highly educational. I am learning to suffer." p. 46

"You cannot imagine how time…can be…so still.
It hangs. It weighs. And yet there is so little of it. It goes so slowly, and yet it is so scarce.
If I were writing this scene, it would last a full fifteen minutes. I would lie here, and you would sit there.
[*She looks at the audience, daring them.*]
Not to worry. Brevity is the soul of wit. But if you think eight months of cancer treatment is tedious for the audience, consider how it feels to play my part." p. 51

[*when a possibility of an infection results in being hospitalized in isolation*]
"I am not in isolation because I have cancer, because I have a tumour the size of a grapefruit. No. I am in isolation because I am being treated for cancer. My treatment imperils my health." p. 66

"I could be so powerful." p. 67

"I don't mean to complain, but I am becoming very sick. Very, very sick. Ultimately sick, as it were.
In everything I have done, I have been steadfast, resolute—some would say in the extreme.
Now, as you can see, I am distinguishing myself in illness." p. 73-74

*[after tests/exams/scans and a long day being poked and prodded]*
"My next line is supposed to be something like this: 'It is such a relief to get back to my room after those infernal tests.'
This is hardly true.
It would be a relief to be a cheerleader on her way to Daytona Beach for Spring Break.
To get back to my room after those infernal tests is just the next thing that happens." p. 74-75

"I always want to know more things. I'm a scholar. Or I was when I had shoes, when I had eyebrows." p. 92

"I want to tell you how it feels. I want to explain it, to use my words. It's as if…I can't… There aren't…I'm like a student and this is the final exam and I don't know what to put down because I don't understand the question and I'm running out of time." p. 94-95

"The time for extreme measures has come. I am in terrible pain. Susie says that I need to begin aggressive pain management if I am going to stand it.
'It': such a little word. In this case, I think 'it' signifies 'being alive.'" p. 95

*Wit is really accurate. It is also very interesting, but mostly it is sad. I recommend reading it (or watching it performed if you can) if you want to understand more about the cancer experience.*

## *remembering Beth*

Beth was always sick, for as long as I can remember.

But she never let it get her down. She knitted hats,
kept at her job (helping people), raised a kind family,
made jokes while driving us to school, gardened whenever she could.

She started the neighborhood annual Easter egg hunt, advocated for the neighborhood park,
created a neighborhood crafts group for kids. She drove me to school many times.

She wrote me letters and sent me texts while I was going through treatment. She said I could
always ask her anything. She made me a hat. She was my inspiration, proof that I could get
through everything and live a happy life with a happy family.

I remember when I just got my port, when I was in the middle of radiation treatment (which
she eventually had to stop using because it was doing more harm than good), she was driving
me and her daughter to a party. I asked if, eventually, you stop feeling the port in your chest,
heavy and awkward. She told me she had hers for over two years. She said you get used to it.

I hope she knows how many lives she's touched, how many flowers we planted to remember
her. How I think of her often and curse whatever is above for bringing an early grievance on
this wonderful family, on this wonderful woman.

I think about her when I see paper cranes, when I think about how she said she felt happy
when they were spinning and sparkling in the light. I think about her every time I feel stressed.
I think of the advice she gave me.

She taught me how to stay kind while living through so much terrible.

## *chemo punch card*

Get your chemo punch card
And then go wait in line
It probably will be real bad
But maybe you'll be fine

Just step right on up
And fill your cup
With chemo, pills, abound

Just sit right down
And you'll be found
Unable to stand up

So grab your chemo punch card
And come on down to try
It could be a good experience
And yes, we sometimes lie

Just hold your breath
No shibboleth
You're not allowed to quit

Just deal with it
(Yeah, we're legit)
Don't worry about death

And grab your chemo punch card
For these, you can keep track
You may lose time, but you will find,
You cannot get it back

## *Cancer Anti-Bucket List*

- Chemotherapy
  - Oral
  - IV
- Lose all hair
- Have radiation
  - Have custom plastic face mold
  - Get tattoos
  - Lay on a flat metal table for over two hours without moving
  - Tear a stress ball
- Ride in a wheelchair
  - Drive a wheelchair
- Have a 108-degree fever
- Have the worst veins for IVs
- Have brain surgery (x2)
- Get a VIP tour of St. Jude (including the inpatient floors and isolation room)
- Fill up a barf bag
- Get nosebleeds
- Use a walker
  - Decorate a walker
- Get a blood transfusion (a lot)
- Get a platelet transfusion (like, a lot a lot)
- Anaphylaxis
  - Have a bunch of nurses called into my room
- Have lung surgery
  - Have a chest tube
- Use walking braces
- Use resting braces
- Have a power port
  - Get my port out
  - Get a port again
- Have adrenal insufficiency
- Get a medical ID band
- Get out of IB exams because my cancer came back
- Be unable to donate blood
- Commute between Atlanta and Knoxville for chemo
- Do college classes virtually
- And counting!

## *is there a reason?*

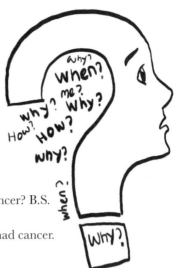

Usually, I feel like nothing happens for a reason.
I'm not religious; I don't believe in a holy purpose or
a prewritten destiny.

I don't think Reasons apply to most things. Disease, poverty,
starvation, war, et cetera, et cetera. Are there Reasons for cancer? B.S.

Maybe I would have accepted Reasons after the first time I had cancer.
The Reasons could have been:

- Learn to value what I have
- Learn how to overcome hardships
- Learn what it's like to go through intense medical treatments as well as experience
  the issues in the American healthcare system
- Be the statistic so someone else doesn't have to be
- Write a really awesome college application essay

Or something like that. I would have been ok with those reasons. "The Shining Example of
what a cancer survivor looks like." Yeah, that would have been me.

But then I had to get cancer AGAIN (and again and again…) and the "Reasons" now tend to
look less and less reasonable. Like, enough already.

But sometimes, I think about the funny nature of Reasons and how things work out. Small
things. Like,

- I leave a binder clip in my bag on accident, then later that day I needed something
  to hold my bag of skittles closed.
- My phone dies right as I am deciding whether or not I should watch another
  YouTube video and keep procrastinating.
- I decide to pop into the dining halls on a night when I'm planning on having
  leftovers, just to see if there is anything worthwhile, and they happen to be serving
  loaded mashed potatoes.
- I go through Tech Green on a day that I normally wouldn't, and I get a free rubber
  duck.

Small coincidences to be sure, but enough to make me think about whether things happen for
a reason.

Probably not, but just a thought.

# CCI (*Childhood Cancer Impatient*)

(*to the tune of "W.I.T.C.H." by Devon Cole*)

She's a childhood cancer impatient

Born in the fall of 2003
Always thought that she would be young, wild, and free
Soon she finds she's spending a long eternity
Hooked up to some fluids and an awful IV

And she don't wanna have to do this again
She's a childhood cancer impatient
And she don't wanna have to deal with the pain
She's a childhood cancer impatient

Always thinks she's done but she's gotta do more
She's got such a vengeful settle to score
She tries to hold it in but lets it out with a roar
Lying on her bedroom and her bathroom floor

And she don't wanna have to do this again
She's a childhood cancer impatient
And she don't wanna have to deal with the pain
She's a childhood cancer impatient

And it's gone on for so long
And it always feels so wrong
Why should she have to write this song?
She's a childhood cancer impatient

'Cause she don't wanna have to do this again
She's a childhood cancer impatient
And she don't wanna have to deal with the pain
She's a childhood cancer impatient

And she don't wanna have to sit in that chair
She's a childhood cancer impatient
And she don't wanna have to lose all her hair
She's a childhood cancer impatient

She's a childhood cancer impatient

## *when I feel alright*

It's funny (in the sense that it is not actually funny, just interesting)
That when I feel good,
It is hard to remember feeling bad.

Somehow, I'm always able to have
An endless stream of optimism
An endless appreciation for the world
A bounce in my step and
An urge to adventure.

I'll say
*When I come back*
*When I see you again*
*I can't wait to do this*
*Next time*
*The same*
*Again*
*Yes*

Words that seem so insignificant to most people,
Experiences people value but not as much knowing they can do it again

I try to value everything, to remember everything
Take pictures, meet people, make memories

How can I feel so hopeful for the future right now when
I know I could feel bad again tomorrow, or the next day?

I don't know.

Somehow the beauty of everything takes over my doubts and fears, and I feel alright.

*bucket hat*

I don't know why, but I feel beautiful right now,
Sitting on the floor of my room, surrounded by boxes to unpack,
Wearing a wrinkled green bucket hat that has white flowers on it.

My eyelashes are thin again,
My hair is sparse and patchy,
My stomach hurts and my ears are ringing.

But I pulled this hat out of a box and I put it on my head
And a laugh bubbled out of my aching chest
As I looked in the mirror and I saw my green bucket hat and its white flowers.

I think the hat pulled the green out of my eyes,
Making a halo around my face where my hair should be,
The white flowers reminding me of a warm spring.

I feel beautiful in my bucket hat,
At midnight in my quiet room,
For no reason at all.

## *cancer playlist pt. 4: songs for when I want to feel better*

"Growing Pains" by Alessia Cara

"The Outsider" by Lyn Lapid

"Talk to Me" by Cavetown

"it's ok!" by Corook

"It's Alright to Cry" by Rosy Grier from *Free to Be...You and Me*

"You Will Be Found" from *Dear Evan Hansen*

"Closer to Fine" by Indigo Girls

"My Silver Lining" by First Aid Kit

"Here Comes the Sun" by The Beatles

"It Gets Better" by Salem Ilese

"Smile" by Johnny Stimson

"Sun Is Gonna Shine" from *Bright Star*

"If We Have Each Other" by Alec Benjamin

"Stepping Stone" by Chase Goehring

"Both Sides Now" cover by Emilia Jones from *CODA*

"O-o-H Child" by Five Stairsteps

"Stand by Me" by Ben E. King

"Down to Earth" by Peter Gabriel

"I Lived" by OneRepublic

"Over the Rainbow" by Israel Kamakawiwo'ole

# *a sunflower goodbye*

Sunflower day fades into night
Yellow petals darken deep out of sight
The Lady slowly sits down to write
The first of her many goodbyes.

Sunflowers can come back every year
Given water, sun, and the best land near,
But sometimes only seeds are here
So take them beneath these skies.

A seed is such a curious thing
A piece of the soul from which they bring
The songs of love that she did sing
And the ones that she implies.

Take these seeds when the raindrops fall
And use them not to build a wall
But instead as a way to call
Or remember where she lies.

For each of you, I leave a seed
For you to have whenever you need
A memory to hold and to read
A final verse of my reprise.